D1568497

Clarence Darrow's Unlikely Friend

Clarence True Wilson

Debaters but always friends

Clarence Darrow's Unlikely Friend

Clarence True Wilson

Debaters but always friends

Robert Dean McNeil

Robert Dean McNeil

Spirit Press
Portland, Oregon

Copyrighted 2007 by Robert Dean McNeil

All rights reserved.
Printed in the USA

ISBN 1-893075-33-8
Library of Congress Number: 2006937663

Cover Art and Design by Debi Vann
Book Design by Larry Foltz

This book may not be reproduced by electronic or any other means which exist now or may yet be developed, without permission of Spirit Press, except in the case of brief quotations embodied in critical articles and reviews.

Spirit Press
www.spiritpress.org
PO Box 12346
Portland, Oregon 97212

Special thank you to those who helped in the first edition of the book.

Maribeth Collins for making available papers of her father to be used in this research project.

Dr. Kenneth E. Rowe, Professor of Church History, Drew University, and Librarian, Methodist Archives and History Center, for supervision of this research project.

Asa Mundell Photos for photo reproductions.

Special thanks to typists Muriel Walker and Pam Nord, and to proof-reader Ruhama Organ. Also thanks to Drew University graduate students Sarah D. Brooks Blair and Leicester Longden for preliminary review of the Wilson papers at the Methodist Archives and History Center.

Robert Dean McNeil
Portland, Oregon Winter 2007

Dedication

Dedicated to my wife, Sara Ann Welch McNeil who for over fifty years has encouraged me to get out and explore the world in search of new truths.

Table of Contents

Introduction

Unlikely Friends

Research for a biography of the Rev. Dr. Clarence True Wilson led me to an interest, admiration and friendship with Clarence Darrow. What a remarkable friendship that developed between prohibition advocate Wilson and the famous defense attorney and agnostic Clarence Darrow. He was a man who set the moral compassion for this nation for fifty years. Would that we had such a moral leader today, be they Christian or agnostic.

A relative of Wilson told me that before Wilson first debated Darrow on the subject of prohibition, he went to the Darrow apartment in Chicago to meet his opponent. Darrow was not at home. His wife Ruby greeted the Rev. Dr. Wilson at the door. When she found out who he was, she said, "I cannot possibly know what you and my husband would have in common."

Further research would indicate that this account may have been purely anecdotal; nevertheless it does speak to the unlikely friendship that did develop during their forty-six debates over a period of five or more years. Not only a friendship between the two men, but between Ruby Darrow and Maude Wilson.

Darrow believed that we human beings are deeply influenced in our adult behavior by the nurturing, or lack of it, by our parents and by the environment which we experience during our childhood. Both Darrow and Wilson were deeply influenced by their fathers. Darrow's father was the town atheist. Wilson's father was a Methodist minister and prohibition advocate. In both cases parenting set the course of their adult lives.

Billy Graham has said, looking back on his ministry, that he wished he had read more Bible. Perhaps clergy would be better informed by reading more biography and great literature. It is in the stories of people's lives that we come, as the Quakers say, "to find that of God in each one." The lives of people like Helen Keller, Gandhi, Nelson Mandela, Martin Luther King Jr., Paul Robeson, Clarence Darrow and so many others speaks truth and morality in the face of adversity every bit as much as the Bible, and other scriptures of the great world religions.

Darrow was a student of the Bible, but he was also a student of Robert Burns, Walt Whitman, Leo Tolstoy, Omar Khayyam, and A. E. Housman. Their lives and writings as well as the influence of his father, the town atheist, were to set the course for his life as an orator, debater and highly respected defense attorney.

It is a credit to Wilson that while he held opposing view points to those of Darrow, he came to admire him, as he was able to understand what motivated him. The two men became best friends. Hopefully the reader of this biography of Wilson will be able to appreciate this remarkable friendship between a preacher and an agnostic. Even as Wilson came to understand and appreciate the moral values held by his opponent, may the reader too learn from Darrow's example and apply some of his wisdom to our present day issues. Darrow was a statesman of the world. He did not believe in God, but he told Wilson, "If there is a God, I believe he would be an internationalist."

The Serenity Prayer

God grant me the serenity to accept the things I cannot change, courage to change the things I can, and wisdom to know the difference.

—Reinhold Niebuhr

Foreword

Clarence True Wilson was my father, and I adored him. He had a kind of personal magnetism which made anything you did with him take on a special magical quality. He died when I was 20, and the world has never seemed quite the same without him.

In some ways he almost seemed like two people—the fervent, courageous crusader whose statements could sometimes sound harsh and judgmental, as opposed to the gentle, accepting, understanding man in all his many personal relationships. He was compassionate and never judgmental—a loving, understanding father; an always devoted husband; a warm, loyal friend. That is perhaps shown best in his friendship with Clarence Darrow, with whom he disagreed on almost everything. During their tour of debates all over the country, they could attack each other fiercely on the platform—then sit up for hours afterward genially discussing these issues as friends.

My father could also let harsh criticism from the press just run off— or greet it with humor—much better than we who loved him could.

Over the years I have thought that someone should write his story, and so I was delighted when Bob McNeil became fascinated by his life and work and wanted to do it.

No one today seems to have a good word to say for Prohibition, but I hope in reading this story that you can look at it in the context of its day, voted in hopefully by a majority of Americans who believed this would solve the alcohol problem. But, with or without Prohibition, the alcohol problem is still with us.

I grew up feeling that the quality I most admired in human beings was dedication and commitment to something one believes in, and my father, in large measure, certainly had that.

Maribeth Wilson Collins

If a Negro did anything to a white man, it was jail or the penitentiary.

– 1 –

Influences of Father on Son

Clarence True Wilson was born at Milton, Sussex County, Delaware, April 24, 1872, the son of the Rev. Dr. John A. B. and Mary Jefferson Wilson. Young Clarence was the ninth generation of the Wilson family to be born in the town of Milton and the eleventh generation of the Jefferson family to be born in Sussex County. The Wilson family was of English, Irish, and Welsh descent. On his mother's side, the Jefferson's were English descendents of the Thomas Jefferson family. Clarence was the first child of a family of four sons and one daughter. He received his middle name, True, from the author of a volume on the Elements of Logic, which was his father's favorite study. Charles K. True was a New England philosopher whose books lined the shelves of the Wilson study. Clarence used his middle name with pride throughout his lifetime. His colleagues of later years sometimes referred to him respectfully as "See True" Wilson.

John A. B. Wilson was one of the most interesting and romantic figures to come upon the American pulpit and platform. He was in the Methodist pulpit before the age of 20 with an unbroken career of rapid promotion, magnetic leadership, and marvelous usefulness in every pastorate, a Presiding Elder (now

District Superintendent) at the early age of 34. He served nine years as a Presiding Elder because of his unlimited capacity for continued labor. Prominent in many reform movements for years, he was at the center of religious, philanthropic, and temperance work in Delaware, Maryland, and Virginia.

It was while his oldest boy was only 2 years old that John Wilson became pastor of the Methodist Episcopal Church in Leipsic, Delaware, where the rum shop was supreme and the churches were on the retreat. In addition to regular parish duties, young Dr. Wilson threw himself into temperance work. On one occasion he stormed the saloon after midnight on Sunday morning with an officer, to command order and to rescue some beaten-up men. He was struck from behind with a ten-pound weight concealed in a handkerchief, and for three or four days he did not regain consciousness. It was one of those early near-martyrdoms that the temperance reformers frequently suffered. (1)

Clarence loved his father dearly. He patterned his life after this unusual crusader of temperance reform.

John Wilson was a sailor from early childhood. His father was a master mariner, who placed his son on board his vessel during vacations and subjected him, at the age of 10, to all the hardships and duties of a sailor boy. Shipwrecked at age 15, at 18 he was first-mate and a very effective one, especially with unmanageable crews.

From this time until his 19th year, John followed the sea. His periods of service gradually lengthened until all his time was spent on the water. He steadily advanced through all the grades from ordinary and able seaman to first-mate. His firmness, frankness, strength, and early maturity made him a leader, and, had he continued in this calling, he would have been a master before his majority.

At the age of 18, John Wilson was converted at a New York City revival conducted by the Rev. W. B. Walton. This impetuous, high-tempered sailor became at once a diligent student of the gospel and a lay preacher. He soon received a wire at New York instructing him to leave the vessel and go to Delaware to take charge of a Methodist circuit of sixteen churches. In no time revivals flared up; war was made on the saloons, and every one of them put out of business on his big circuit— a characteristic of his ministry in other places.

John Wilson was an avid, eager student and read thoroughly every book within his reach. In December 1867, he entered the academy at Milton, Delaware, and completed the course as valedictorian of his class. Following his calling from the sea to a Methodist circuit, Dr. Wilson was appointed a junior preacher on the Sharptown, Delaware circuit in 1868 and for nearly a year conducted extensive and successful revivals. In 1869, he joined the Wilmington Conference of the Methodist Episcopal Church and was stationed at Millsboro on the Lewis circuit. Here and at Harrington, where he transferred in 1870, many converts were made to the church through his preaching, and in 1871 he was admitted to full clergy membership and ordained elder by Bishop Levi Scott. (2)

Clarence's mother, Mary Elizabeth Jefferson Wilson, was born in 1850 in Georgetown, Delaware, and died September 26, 1930. Loved, trusted, admired by a wide circle of friends, she joined the Methodist Episcopal Church at an early age. The Wilsons were married in 1870 when she was 20 and he was 22. John at one time served a sixteen-point circuit and led revival meetings at other churches, sometimes as many as ten months out of the year. Mary could go with him and board or stay home alone. Most often she went with him and helped him in every department of his work.

Following pastorates in Delaware and Maryland in 1875, John Wilson moved to Boston where he became pastor of the famous Father Taylor's Bethel Mission. At the time, this was one of the most famed church-sponsored institutions for sailors in the world. By this time there were two small boys in the Wilson family.

Mrs. Wilson organized a Temperance Society and secured pledges. During their two-year pastorate in Boston in 1875-1876, over 700 people were converted at the altar and 25,000 signed the total abstinence pledge, including sailors from all over the world and students from the universities of Boston. Mrs. Wilson taught Bible classes, including a class of 150 sailors every Sunday, while she was in Boston. The severity of the weather made it difficult for her or the children to remain through the winter. Two years later the Wilsons returned to take up ministerial duties in northeast Maryland.

After two years, Dr. Wilson was sent to the Asbury Methodist Episcopal Church in Wilmington, Delaware, and from there, to Fairmount, Maryland, from 1880 to 1883. By this time there were four boys in the family. A daughter had died after living only eight months.

Dr. Wilson's intense public life was made possible in part by his wife, who took domestic cares and perplexities entirely off his mind. Mrs. Wilson was also gifted in prayer, the reading of Bible passages, and the telling of Bible stories.

The years at Fairmount were of special interest to Clarence and his younger brothers. Clarence True Wilson later wrote a tribute to his father's ministry at Fairmount called "The Fighter of Fairmount." A digest of this account provides a portrait of the older Wilson as seen through the eyes of the preacher's oldest son:

> *The Delmarva Peninsula, a part of the Atlantic seaboard jutting down into the ocean and bordered by the Delaware Bay on the East and the Chesapeake on the West, includes all of Delaware and the eastern shores of Maryland and Virginia. On the Chesapeake Bay side of this peninsula is a little scattered community once known as "Potato Neck" but later named more euphoniously Fairmount, probably because it was not fair and there was no mount.*
>
> *When we moved there in 1880, we had lived in Boston and in Wilmington. We packed our goods and took the down state train through Delaware into the Eastern Shore of Maryland. Fairmount was seven miles off the Eastern*

Shore of Maryland. Fairmount was seven miles off any railroad and there were no telephones. The roads were hard and dusty in summer and bottomless in winter. The cold weather was breaking and we wondered how we would reach our destination. We looked out of the window and heard the conductor call out "Eden" and mother burst into tears as she saw that forlorn station, and cried, "If this is Eden what must Fairmount be?"

We had passed Salisbury and were now nearing the aristocratic little county-seat town of Princess Anne, and soon after, we heard the longed for name of "Westover." This was the railroad station nearest Fairmount. We beheld a top wagon drawn by a pair of mules—"Jack" and "Mouse." Mr. "Sammy" Hall had been sent by a hospitable people to convey the new "Methodist Preacher and his folks" to Fairmount and the well stored, well lighted parsonage, where dinner had been provided and the larder stored for many days.

We boys found an ample yard of one and a half acres. Great oak trees gave shade in summer and bedding for horse and cow in winter.

Did nature ever concentrate so many of her charms in one locality? The Peninsula has no mountains, or wild scenery, but it has ocean shores, two world-famed bays, and rivers that wind and intertwined, and the homes of the prosperous people face these beautiful little streams.

Rabbits were plentiful and we made traps

and caught many, each giving us a great thrill as of a conqueror. In the mild season of the year boating, fishing, and crabbing of Hall's creek held us boys enthralled.

At that time the malaria was rife in Fairmount. The tide would overflow the swamps, settle in pools, breed mosquitoes and they would swarm so thick that I have seen them darken the roadway so it would trouble one to see the horse he was driving and blind one to every team or rig that was coming down the road. It was not uncommon to hear "A horse got mired in the marsh and before anyone could find him in the morning, he was killed—bled to death by mosquitoes."

Intermittent fever, malarial fever, typhoid fever raged in the community incessantly. The Methodist Church had sixty funerals one summer, and nothing was done about the condition.

The people of Fairmount took their religion and their politics seriously. The opposition would fight at the drop of a hat or a chip from the shoulder. There were three stores, each of them centers of their respective clans.

The subjects that ruled the politics were Local Option and White Supremacy. The community divided on whether a "nigger" had any rights that a white man was bound to respect. And the community had long settled that in the negative. It was a favorite trick to find a colored man in trouble, bail him out, pay the lawyer or court costs and have him sign away his services till the debt was paid. In this way the white man had a slave for years without having to buy him.

A Negro woman, named Eliza, lost her husband. She was left alone with a little seven-year-old daughter. During her husband's illness of some month's duration, the H. Clay Tull store supplied her groceries. It looked like a fine charity! But the inevitable pay day came. H. Clay Tull and "Doc" Dickinson drove down to the little cabin home and demanded payment immediately, if not sooner. There was no money. Eliza took in washing, but her white neighbors had not paid promptly. Then she must give up her daughter and bind her over to H. Clay Tull till the debt was paid. She was told the law required it. She signed by making her mark before the witness brought for the purpose. No provision was made for ever seeing her little girl—not once a week, or once a month, or once a year. The screaming child was put into the buggy between the two men and driven away. Weeks passed and this widow, bereft of husband and now of child, went to the store, but no sight of her daughter was vouchsafed. The mother told sympathizing friends she didn't know whether "Sophie" was dead or alive. The suspense deepened the apprehension. One Sunday afternoon the child slipped out of the house to run away to her mother. Instinct drew the mother to start for the white slave-owner's house to recapture her daughter. They met at the back gate, and hand in hand, made their way the two miles over fields and woods to the humble home.

The child was missed. The inseparable pair, Doc Dickinson and H. Clay Tull, loaded a shot gun for this mother and drove post haste to the cabin. They called for her to come out and bring "Sophie." She appeared in the doorway with a hoe to protect her home and child. The heroic leader of the brave pair drew the shot gun and fired it point blank at this mother. She fell in her own doorway and the other companion ran around the back way and caught the screaming child, snatching her from her stricken mother and desolated home. Though one of the men was a doctor, Eliza was left in her blood and would soon have bled to death but for colored neighbors who secured the service of the other doctor of the town—Dr. C. W. Miles.

The Magistrate fined the two one dollar and twenty cents each for this deed. That was his usual fine for bootleggers whom the community brought before him —that is, if the case was perfectly clear and there was no way of clearing them outright.

The church sometimes had good meetings. It depended on whether the preacher was muscular enough to make the sons of Belial wish to let him proceed. But misbehavior in church was characteristic of the meetings, and "bush" meetings generally provoked disorder, such as pulling the pegs out of one side of the boards on which the sets rested so that, when the preacher was midway his appeal, a sharp shove and fifty people would land on the ground.

Seats were placed across till a thousand people could be seated before the platform for preacher and choir. The meetings were held at night, but there were neither electric lights nor gas, so a square box was built for the lighting of a huge fire so that the faces of the preacher and the choir could be seen by the crowd. If the meeting got to going so as to really threaten to invade the ranks of the unregenerate, their leaders would slip in and conceal a hand full of powder in the earth under the fire. When the meeting was in progress, the fire finally warms through this earthen foundation, and one after another exploding and blazing cinders would fly in all directions. This was but one of the many coarse jokes on the good people who held the only hope of decency in the community.

Strange to say, Fairmount was a dry community. There were however bootleggers abroad in the land. One stayed on the edge of Fairmount and did business on Saturdays in nearby Princess Anne.

Most of the folks in Fairmount voted Democratic. Vote-buying was common. The Democrats would get out a full state and county ticket in the old days with the picture of Abe Lincoln upon it. This would be handed out to the colored people who, seeing the picture, would hasten to vote with a smile of satisfaction on their somber faces, showing the white in their eyes and their whiter teeth. It was easy to get men for five dollars a piece to vote certain ways, then sign the name of the buyer upon the ticket.

The type of politics may be indicated by the Justice of the Peace, who came to Fairmount once a week. His name was James Furnace. He had been appointed by the Governor and had held the office since "the memory of man runneth not to the contrary." If a white man did anything to a Negro, he was generally told "be careful and not disturb the peace any more"; if a Negro did anything to a white man, it was the jail or the penitentiary. If white or black was convicted after long months of immunity of selling liquor without a license, they invariably got a fine of $1.20. This seemed to be the Justice's share of the proceeds and he wasn't extravagant in his other demands. His sympathies were quite as broad and intense for the bootleggers.

What this county and community needed was a master who was not afraid to go up against rum-rule, dirty politics, race prejudice, ruffianism, and general baseness, and give it an alternative, either the Gospel of Love or of Muscular Christianity, whichever the occasion seemed to require.

Another element was interjected when the Wilmington Conference of the Methodists assigned to Fairmount in March 1880, a new pastor in the person of Rev. John A. B. Wilson. He was only thirty. He had been a sailor in early life and the first mate of a sailing vessel at nineteen. Wilson, his wife and sons and his wife's two younger sisters, Cora and Sue, all came into Fairmount on that memorable March night in the chill of a breaking winter and in the dark of a community that had never known the street lamp.

The preacher and his family were met in the warm parsonage by as warm-hearted people as ever supported a minister in his benevolent and reformatory work for a community. They liked their ministers, especially if they did not run afoul of their politics and their superstitions.

Very soon the community discovered that a new pastorate of energy, force, vision, progressiveness, and reform had been set up among them. This man actually called a Negro man "brother" and tipped his hat when he spoke to a Negro woman. Whenever a Negro was arrested for assault and battery, Wilson would appear, and if he knew the man, he would testify to his good moral character—a thing that a white man had never done before under similar circumstances.

He occasionally would go down and preach in the Colored Church believing that his gospel would not be contaminated by its exposure to the color that predominated there. Whenever a question was in dispute regarding the rights of the weaker race he was generally for the weaker against the dominant one, and when a fight was to occur—being very handy with his fists—he has been known to step in and attack a dozen men when a forlorn Negro boy was all there was on the other side.

He discovered that some of the young men converted in his church were getting liquor. They learned that at a place called Jamestown there was a man by the name of Tom Dryden who ran a blind-pig establishment. The term, "bootlegger," was not then so popular and they called them blind pigs and blind tigers. The preacher used to say that he preferred a blind pig or a blind tiger to one with both eyes open—especially if it was after his boy, but he didn't know why they should call an unlicensed liquor seller by the name of an animal—unless he be named a "skunk" which is the animal that dispenses strong liquor without a license. So a young man of his Bible class went up and got plenty of evidence against this bootlegger in Jamestown, three miles north of the Methodist Church. To convict a man before that magistrate required a mathematical demonstration, an ocular revelation, an overwhelming list of witnesses, and a group of determined spectators with fire in their eyes. The case was closed and the man who had been running on for years convicted, but Justice of the Peace Furnace withheld the sentence until the next day and sent word down that the sentence was $1.20 fine.

This put the preacher on his neck! At the close of the Wednesday night prayer meeting the pastor called all the men into his study. It was decided to go up and remove the building where the liquor was stored and being sold contrary to law. The men were to take the women home and assemble at the parsonage at eleven o'clock that night. Twenty-five men joined the pastor and began driving their rigs toward the bootlegging establishment. A half mile before reaching the place they stopped and cut down a couple of trees to use as battering rams to batter that bootlegging building into nonentity.

But the fighting parson was tender hearted; he always put himself in the other fellow's place. He began to think of that mother and children; so he said: "Men, you get the battering rams ready while I go up and get the mother and children out of the building." He knocked on the door. The woman came to the door, and seeing his face exclaimed: "Oh, Mr. Wilson, I am so glad you came. My husband is very ill, and I have felt like sending for you all evening. Won't you come upstairs and pray for my husband." In two minutes he is in the sick room receiving the confessions of a man very ill. He asks for prayer. The pastor is on his knees by the bedside of the bootlegger; the man is genuinely penitent and according to the old-established Methodist's faith and practice is converted. He says, "I want you to help me roll the whiskey barrels out of my basement and have a bonfire; I am through with liquor selling forever." The men were called in to help remove the whiskey and a bonfire blazed that could be seen for miles around.

The town had but one doctor and he proved a cruel and uncaring person. People were dying of most anything. Who expected ever to get well of pneumonia, typhoid, or intermittent fever, or diphtheria, or scarlet fever. Send for the preacher and prepare for the funeral.

Most men would leave a condition like that; but not that preacher. He wrote to the President of Boston University, described the "conditions of health and morals and said, "I am going to do the minister's part down here, but I need a trained, experienced, and skillful physician. Won't you find one? I will guarantee his support." In a short time Dr. Gill, of Boston, appeared. He was only to look over the field; but the pastor took him in a single day to see the sick,—fifteen patients his first day. He never got back to Boston. "Incurable" patients began to recover. The preacher was now blessed not only as a soul saver, but as a life saver. There is more than one way in which an intelligent progressive can help a conservative community.

The Wilmington Conference was to open in Cambridge, Maryland March 20, 1883. The venerable Bishop Simpson, friend of Lincoln, patriot, prophet, the greatest preacher of his century, was to preside. Three Presiding Elders of the Conference were to be appointed. The Salisbury District was to have a new leader. The district embraced the lower counties of the Eastern Shore of Maryland, a good section of lower Delaware, and the two counties of the

Eastern Shore of Virginia. It was border territory. The war might be over but the reconstructive period had left its unhealed wound. Southern sympathizers would sometimes tell Northern preachers, "You are not wanted here."

It was to this district that John A. B. Wilson was appointed Presiding Elder in March 1883. He chose for his place of residency the aristocratic old town of Princess Anne. It was a town of choice families and high ideals with fine schools and cultured church life. But the wealthy people of the town were not Methodists and they did not want this Negro advocate and temperance agitator in their midst. There were seven or eight houses available in the little town of eight hundred inhabitants. But when the new appointee started out to rent a place, it was startling to find how they had each just been rented. A group of business men had pooled funds and rented by the month every vacant house in town. These aristocrats wished for peace at any price.

Wilson had the wit to win this battle. He needed a four year lease in order serve out the term of his appointment. He found a colored man who was a local restaurant keeper who had a four year lease and asked if he could buy out his lease and pay his moving expense to move to any one of the other houses that could be rented by him in the town. Wilson asked Mr. Maddox: "What will you sell me this lease for if I pay your moving expenses?" "Mr. Wilson, you have done so much for my people that you could have my house if I had to move out and sleep in the county road. You can have it by simply paying the rent."

The family moved into this house. It was owned by the leader of the opposition, but the Wilsons had the lease. For four years that was the center of the history-making of the peninsula. Twenty-six new churches where none existed before were planned for and planted to grow. Revivals of far-reaching influence swept the Salisbury District with an average of twenty-four hundred conversions each year.

During those militant days as Presiding Elder of the Salisbury District, the Pennsylvania Railroad decided to extend its Delaware and Maryland branch down into Accomack and Northampton counties of Virginia. It was in this territory that every Northern Methodist preacher with two or three exceptions had been driven out during the state of bad feelings subsequent to the Civil War.

The Presiding Elder followed the survey and the laying out of the towns and planted a Methodist Church in every town with a prospect of becoming more than a station, started Sunday Schools wherever there was cross-roads settlement, organized classes for probationers, the nucleus of churches.

The end of the road was at Cape Charles, already a considerable town. The fame of this militant Presiding Elder preceded him. It was rumored that he was coming down there to preach. He had friends go to the pastors of the several churches, but "no" was the uniform answer. They applied for the school house. At once objections were lodged. On his arrival, he asked for the hotel porch. It was granted, but the grant was soon rescinded. It was cold weather, a house of some kind was needed or a service could not well be held. It went around the town that the Presiding Elder was completely blocked; no one would let him preach in any place.

But the leading saloon keeper heard it, and remembering that his mother had been a Methodist, came to the hotel, sought out the Methodist Preacher and said, "If you would honor my saloon by preaching in it, you can turn my bar into a pulpit. I will set it with a hundred chairs and get up a congregation." It was just the opportunity this militant man would have coveted. He accepted the proposal instantaneously. The saloon-keeper went into the bottom of his trunk, got out the Bible that his mother had given him, which had suffered no wear and tear since, put a nice cover over the bar, laid a Bible and some hymn books on it, the place was properly set and the crowds began to come. Mr. Wilson was at his best. He sang his favorite hymn:

"Arise, my soul, arise;
Shake off thy guilty fears,
A bleeding sacrifice
In thy behalf appears,"

> *knelt, and offered a prayer that would have moved a heart of stone, and did melt all the stony hearts. Everybody wept; some wept aloud. He read three or four favorite passages of Scripture that reminded many of them of their early training; preached on "Come unto me all ye that labor and are heavy laden and I will give you rest. Take my yoke upon you and learn of me, for I am meek and lowly of heart and you shall find rest for your souls."*
>
> *When he gave the invitation, forty-five stalwart men turned both sides of that bar into an altar. A class meeting was organized with the saloon-keeper as class leader. Another bon-fire occurred when barroom fixtures and whiskey barrels went up in flame, and several things were accomplished—a saloon was put out of business peaceably; a Methodist Episcopal Church was organized; a racial, sectional, and religious prejudice was allayed, and in two nights half a hundred souls were converted to the living of the Christian life. And when one sees beautiful Cape Charles, Virginia, a city of lovely homes and thriving churches and schools, and wonders how they were planted, he can take this story as the origin of the First Methodist Episcopal Church of Cape Charles, Virginia. (3)*

In writing of his father's fighting years in Fairmount and Princess Anne, Clarence tells how he and his brothers enjoyed play in the woods, along the rivers, and on the seashores of the Maryland coast. Mostly, however, he seemed to enjoy the company of older persons. While his father was Presiding Elder in the Wilmington Conference and they lived at Princess Anne, young Wilson grew in years from age 10 to 14. He writes, "As a boy I sought the society of older people and was honored with the friendship of one who was considered the best-read and most revered citizen of the town, Mr. Samuel Colonna, a wheel-wright, who for forty years was a justice of the peace."

The date was April 24, 1886. "Clarence, so you are 14 years old today, are you? You are 14 and I am over 40. Little doubt you will be living long after I am gone. I am going to trust you with a secret." The secret was an amazing account of the escape of John Wilkes Booth. This conversation was to start Clarence on a life-long adventurous hobby in seeking the answer to the question: "Was John Wilkes Booth shot to death in Garrett's burning barn, or did he escape to live on for thirty-eight years, dying a suicide death in Enid, Oklahoma?"

At the age of 16 Clarence spent his spare time in a lawyer's office reading through Blackstone and Kent's commentaries. About this time, however, he was converted and felt himself called to the ministry. A few nights after his conversion, he was called upon to speak in his church before a crowded congregation. A revival started which resulted in the conversion of many. Being called upon for a similar service elsewhere, Clarence was soon in the midst of a marked career as a boy preacher. (4) An early account of Dr. Wilson's life in Prohibition Leaders in America reports that he was converted and joined the church at the age of 11. His first sermon, preached at the Concord camp meeting in Caroline County, Maryland, before he was 16, created a deep impression. (5) Here is Dr. Wilson's own reporting of that event:

> *I was invited to speak at Lewis, Delaware, at a great out-of-door meeting in the interest of local option. My father was to deliver the principal address and they wanted me to come and make the first speech. Considering the occasion important, I began a careful preparation by writing out what I had to say. The first sentence I ever wrote was this: "There is a traffic in our midst which bears upon its face the curse of God and the blood of men." I was rather pleased with this opening sentence and, with that start, did pretty well. A few days later my father returned and asked how I was getting along with the preparation for my speech. I told him I would read it to him. I started out with great gusto, reading the first sentence, which I thought pretty good, and on and on I went until the speech was concluded. Finally, I said to Father, "How do you like it?"*
>
> *"Very well."*
>
> *"How do you like that first sentence?"*
>
> *"Well," he said, "modesty would prevent my praising that overmuch."*
>
> *I flushed and wondered. He said, "Did you ever read your Papa's sermon on "The Blood Traffic and Its Concomitants?"*
>
> *"No, I never did."*

"Did you know I had it published in pamphlet form?"

"No, I have never seen a pamphlet of the kind."

Father went to the desk and, opening a drawer, handed me "The Blood Traffic and Its Concomitants." To my amazement this discourse opened with the words: "There is a traffic in our midst which bears upon its face the blood of men and the curse of God." I had never read it, never seen it, but when I was a little boy of five, the date of the preparation of this sermon, it was quite common for me to lie on the floor on a big blanket, with blocks and paints and other things and work at my things while listening to my father read over his preparation for sermons. I have no doubt that that sentence thus lodged in my mind and as subconsciously as anything was ever reproduced, I imagined that I had produced an original sentence. (6)

At the age of 15 Clarence moved with his parents to Dover, Delaware, and while attending school preached regularly with great success to the convicts in the state prison. (7)

He was called upon to preach in the neighboring churches and was soon known as a popular preacher and lecturer. Crowds flocked to hear him, especially at camp meeting. The evils of drink, gambling, and vice soon became apparent to the brilliant youth. He was made state lecturer for the "Good Templars" and canvassed Delaware in their interest for the cause of abstinence and prohibition.

> He was secretary of the Delaware State Central Committee of the Prohibition Party, and stumped the State for candidate Fisk. Everywhere he was stationed vigorous temperance work was done and success achieved. (8)

"Tall, graceful, manly, serious, thoughtful, earnest, logical, eloquent" is how the press described the effects of his ministry. He was often called the "Boy Preacher." He was appointed pastor at Rising Sun, Delaware, and at age 17, a summer supply at his father's Eighteenth Street Methodist Episcopal Church in New York at age 18 and 19. During his 19th year he pastored in the large town of Seaford, Delaware. From the time he was 20 to 23, he was pastor in the New York Conference at Sea Cliff on Long Island.

An editorial in the *Seaford News* referred to his transfer from Seaford to Long Island.

> The Wilmington Conference loses in this transfer the most remarkable young preacher that was ever connected with it. Mr. Wilson, though but twenty years of age, is well and favorably known, and his services are very much sought after. Through the persistent entreaties of the church, he has remained until this time. Never in her history has the church enjoyed such prosperity or won such success. The church has been unified, the congregation

> has grown until every available space is occupied, old and troublesome debts have been paid, the benevolences have been greatly advanced and a sweeping revival was enjoyed last winter. If Mr. Wilson could remain here another year, every indication points to the building of a new church, the lot for which has been secured free of debt. In this transfer we lose, and New York gains one of Delaware's most brilliant and beloved sons. (9)

During these years Clarence was ordained deacon at the early age of 18, and elder at age 20, the youngest man ever ordained in the Methodist Episcopal Church, so it was reported. He was educated in the high school of Princess Anne, Maryland, at the Wilmington Conference Academy in Dover, Delaware, and at St. John's College, Annapolis, Maryland. He was 17 when he entered St. John's College, Annapolis, and was taking charge of churches near the college. He organized a Young Men's Christian Association in the school and was its president throughout his course of study. Thomas Fell, president of St. John's College, paid tribute to student Wilson:

> Dr. Clarence True Wilson was a student of St. John's College in 1890 and at that time manifested considerable power as an orator and public speaker. Since that time I have heard him preach on several occasions, when he clearly showed that he had developed to a high degree his natural gift of eloquence. (10)

Clarence's study was frequently interrupted and at last broken off before graduation by the imperative demands for his ministry. At Sea Cliff, such revivals broke out that the congregation was compelled to enlarge the church to accommodate the crowds which flocked to his ministry, and the membership tripled. At age 22, Clarence was invited to an important church of his denomination, the Sixty-First Street Methodist Episcopal Church, New York City, but he was compelled to decline due to poor health. (11)

That young man will go back east in a box.

— 2 —

From Delaware to California (1895-1904)

In the year 1895, when Clarence was a young man of 23 years, his health broke so completely that it was decided he would have to move to California in an attempt to regain his health. He and his mother took the long train trip through the southern states to southern California. It was an interesting trip, which his mother detailed in a diary of their travels. She was impressed by the beautiful scenery along the way. She was shocked at the large number of poor black persons living in the South. "We find the curse of drinking everywhere," she confided in her diary.

When Mrs. Wilson and her son arrived at the depot in Los Angeles, two men standing by saw how sickly Clarence appeared. One remarked to the other, "That young man will go back to the east in a box." He was to prove them wrong. The climate helped greatly to improve his health. Soon he was continuing his schooling and not long after resumed his preaching and temperance work. By the year 1898 he had written and published his first book.

The book, published in December 1898, was entitled *The Things That Are To Be: Pulpit Discussions in Eschatology*. Eschatological issues were to be a matter of great interest to Clarence throughout his lifetime. He was especially interested in the prophecy of Isaiah regarding the ten lost tribes of Israel. He believed that this was a prophecy of the special role of the Anglo-Saxon people as the Ten Lost Tribes of Israel, called in the present day to a special evangelistic mission to proclaim Christ's teaching throughout the world. The book was written while he was pastor of the North Pasadena Methodist Episcopal Church.

While in California Clarence completed his college and seminary education. He received a bachelor of arts degree from the University of Southern California, at the time a Methodist school. He was elected to Phi Beta Kappa while there. He also received the degree of bachelor of philosophy from San Joaquin Valley College and a degree in theology from Maclay College of Theology. He was later to receive an honorary doctor of divinity degree from St. John's College in the year 1900 and an honorary doctor of laws degree from Washington College, Chesterton, Maryland, in 1926.

The Maclay College of Theology was established in 1887 by Charles Maclay. Maclay had been a young minister in Pennsylvania, a field representative for Methodist-related Dickinson College in Carlisle and for the Lycoming College at Williamsport, when he felt the call at the mid-century to go into a more active and far-reaching engagement in the mission of the church.

On January 7, 1851, Charles Maclay accepted an invitation to missionary service in California. On

March 28 he and his bride of a few days left New York on a difficult sea journey, crossing Panama by mule, and continuing by the Pacific. They entered San Francisco harbor on May 5, 1851. Maclay labored for a time among the pioneers, doing missionary work, and then went into business. He at first did well in business activities. As a result, after a decade of labor in California, he was able to make a significant gift in behalf of education for the ministry. The annual Methodist Conference in 1885 received a report of a gift of a ten-acre campus and a fifteen-room building in San Fernando, which was to be a school of theology. This school became a part of the University of Southern California system of educational institutions, but remained affiliated with the Methodist Episcopal Church.

The Maclay College of Theology opened in the autumn of 1887. R.W.C. Farnsworth, one of the presiding elders of the conference, was the first dean. Later, Professor Fletcher B. Cherrington served as acting dean for a time upon the unexpected death of Dean Farnsworth. Robert S. (Sam) Maclay, brother of Charles, was then called home from Japan to be dean. It was noted that the faculty was well equipped through wide experience in educational work in this and "foreign" lands. In view of the focus of interest and experience which was seen in the founding and early formation of the college, it is not surprising that the faculty included persons with competence for instruction in Asian languages, and the concern for the mission of the church was reflected in the curriculum. One of the teachers, Dr. Cochran, had been associated with Maclay in mission work in Japan. Sam

Maclay had also been in China.

The mission in which Charles Maclay had begun his ministry in California had taken a turn of events which could hardly have been imagined. But, just as he had experienced financial gain, he also expe-rienced decline and the school itself fell on difficult times. By June 1891, Dean Maclay was the only member of the faculty. The campus at San Fernando was closed and the property sold. The school was moved to the campus of the College of Liberal Arts of the University of Southern California, Los Angeles. Robert Maclay continued as dean of the College of Theology, offering instruction in religion at the Los Angeles location in 1893-94.

During the ensuing years, when the theological department was not formally operating, courses were offered by George I. Cochran, a layman who returned to the faculty and served as dean from 1894-99. The school was officially closed by vote of the board of trustees from 1899 to 1907. Many years later, these early beginnings in an attempt at theological education by the Methodist Episcopal Church would flower in the establishment in 1957 of the School of Theology at Claremont. (1)

Clarence attended the Maclay College of Theology while also completing his bachelor of arts degree at the University of Southern California. He received his bachelor of arts in 1896 and his bachelor of divinity in 1898. This was during the time that George I. Cochran was dean. Clarence's own poor health, which led to his move to California, and the financial difficulties of this very early attempt to establish a first-rate school of theology in southern California may have robbed young Wilson of a well-rounded theological education.

While Clarence may have been robbed of a solid theological education, he did not lack so far as academic pursuits were concerned. In his teen years, before he began preaching, he read books of law, logic, and philosophy. He studied the Bible and read Bible commentaries. A published author at age 26, he was also a student of history, biography, and political science.

Dr. Wilson was to remain all his life a theological conservative. He held a distrust for "eastern liberal" theological education and especially for the "higher criticism" of German theologians, popular at the turn of the twentieth century. One might wonder what direction his thoughts would have taken if poor health had not forced him to finish his schooling in Southern California. Perhaps he would have come under the influence of one of the eastern schools such as Drew, Boston, Union, Princeton, or Yale. He might have thus had the making of another preaching giant like Tittle or Fosdick.

The strongest influences upon his life work were not theological teachers but temperance reformers. When Dr. Wilson was only 23, he was already considered a national leader in the temperance reform movement. He was listed with several hundred other leaders in a book written by B. T. Austin and published in Canada, titled *Prohibition Leaders in America*. The book was published in 1895 and listed nearly all the great leaders of the temperance movement of the nineteenth century in both the United States and Canada. The first half of the book contains articles about the temperance reform and the second half is made up of pictures and biographical sketches of each of the Prohibition leaders. The book is like a bible for the movement and must have had a great influence on Dr. Wilson's own views regarding temperance and prohibition.

From this book, with its examples of the crusading spirit of Frances Willard, Alden W. Young, Samuel Potter, and others, Dr. Wilson was inspired to join the growing band of temperance reformers. From the lives of nineteenth-century temperance crusaders Dr. Wilson gained his inspiration to become the "Number One Dry" of the twentieth century.

> He became pastor of the North Pasadena Church, and remained for four years there where the saloons were closed by the efforts which he organized and the church membership multiplied by four.
>
> He was transferred to Santa Monica, a city of 15 saloons and four weak churches. Within six months he had secured the closing of all the saloons, passage of an ordinance closing business places on Sunday, and greatly increased the churches by conducting revival services in his church in which the other churches of the city united and many converts joined with the religious forces of the town. He was invited from there to First Church of San Diego, where he conducted a County Local Option campaign, which carried the entire county outside the city limits; and later made a series

> of exposures of objectionable features in the Theosophical Society of Madam Tingley, and for months was the author of numerous discourses, newspaper articles, and magazine essays on the evils he saw in the teachings of Point Loma Theosophy. (2)

From 1901 to 1905, Dr. Wilson was again preaching on the East Coast, this time at St. Luke's Methodist Episcopal Church in Newark, and there he was found battling the liquor interest in the state of New Jersey. One day, soon after arrival in Newark, Dr. Wilson was shopping in a department store in the city when he got off on the wrong floor and entered the wine room. He saw young girls stretched out on sofas or settees with nurses waiting upon them. It looked to him like a hospital. He made a little inquiry and found that the People's Department Stores gave 10 percent of all purchases to girls or women in wine tickets. For $3.00 worth of merchandise, one could go upstairs and spend thirty cents in tickets for liquors of any kind. No questions were asked about age. He saw girls not sixteen years of age stupefied by drink. Though he had been in the city only two months, Dr. Wilson made war on that practice the next Sunday night. He started a petition to the city council, got signatures from the businessmen the next day, and that night, though these stores were represented by able counsel, he made such a presentation of the outrage of this liquor system of tempting young people—who were simply sent on errands by their mothers—to drink, that the licenses of the three People's Stores were revoked forthwith. They then begged for the privilege of running all through the holidays, but as the license was revoked immediately, Dr. Wilson notified them that he would have officers watching them that night and the next day. If another drop of liquor was sold, he would have the proprietor arrested and prosecuted with such an exposure of the kind of hellhole he was running that decent people would cut their patronage of the People's Stores for all purposes. So he started a pastorate of three years with this spectacular and successful move against "demon rum." (3)

In Portland, Oregon Dr. Wilson soon took the lead in social reform work. Wilson was a moderate sized advancer edition of the Day of Judgment.

— 3 —

Oregon Years (1905-1910)

The years at St. Luke's Church in Newark proved successful; membership of the church nearly doubled. But at the end of three years Dr. Wilson's craving for the West and its type of life led him to accept a call to the Grace Methodist Episcopal Church in Portland, Oregon. There he found a family church of earnest people, but a church that had never been effective in either evangelism or civic influence. Dr. Wilson preached his first sermon in Portland on February 19, 1905. Two years later the *Oregon Daily Journal* reported: "It is needless to say that Grace Church, from being one of the most quiet churches in the city, has become one of the most widely known in the state." (1)

In Portland he soon took the lead in social reform work. He headed the campaign in opposition to liquor dealers' amendment but opposed woman suffrage and helped to pile up the 11,000 majority against it. He started the opposition against slot machines which resulting in the removal of those gambling devices, and he aided in the closing of saloons on Sunday. A Portland newspaper reported, "He takes an interest in everything in church and state, and everybody, good and bad, and has an opinion on everything, which he is willing to state at any time with perfect frankness." (2)

A colleague reported: "Dr. Clarence True Wilson is known on the Pacific coast as the fearless champion of all that ought to be, and is justly regarded, by both friends and foes of civic righteousness, as a moderate sized advance edition of the Day of Judgment." (3)

In May of 1907, Dr. Wilson and Dr. J. Whitcomb Brougher, pastor of First Baptist Church, Portland, then known as the White Temple, debated the issue of woman suffrage. Dr. Brougher favored the vote for women. Dr. Wilson was opposed. He was much opposed to women working outside the home or getting into politics. He stated that three-fourths of women did not want to vote. Not only did Dr. Wilson and Dr. Brougher debate the issue of woman suffrage but also on a lighter note, they debated the pros and cons of marriage. Dr. Wilson, being at the time a bachelor, argued in favor of the single life.

In May 1906, soon after Dr. Wilson came to Portland, his father, John A. B. Wilson, died of typhoid fever in Grass Valley, California, where he had been serving as pastor. The older Wilson had had a remarkable pastoral career. In 1884, he was elected alternate delegate to the General Conference of the Methodist Episcopal Church. Four years later he was elected on the first ballot as delegate to the General Conference. In 1887, Dickinson College in Carlisle, Pennsylvania, conferred on him the degree of doctor of divinity. In 1892 he became pastor of the Eighteenth Street Methodist Episcopal Church in New York City where he established a home for working women. He followed his son Clarence to southern California and served churches in Los Angeles and San Francisco before going to Grass Valley. He is listed in the *Cyclopedia of Temperance* with other temperance leaders. (4)

Clarence True Wilson was pastor of Grace Methodist Episcopal Church in Portland from 1905 to 1908. From 1908 to 1910 he served his second pastorate in Portland at Centenary Methodist Episcopal Church. November 28, 1908, he married Maude Akin Tifft, the daughter of founding members of Grace Church. The papers at the time twitted his having been anti-marriage as well as against woman suffrage.

Dr. Wilson was 36 years old at the time of his marriage to Maude Akin Tifft. They loved each other dearly through the years. Dr. Wilson adopted Maude's daughter, Virginia, and later they were to have a second daughter, Mary Elizabeth (Maribeth), named for Clarence's mother, Mary Elizabeth Jefferson Wilson. The Wilsons had a devoted family life. The bond of love and devotion which existed between Dr. and Mrs. Wilson was of a rare quality. Fifty years after their father's death and eighteen years after their mother's death, daughters Virginia and Maribeth still spoke with much affection regarding their parents.

The temperance reform work had begun in Oregon long before Wilson arrived on the scene. The first Oregon Temperance Society was organized by pioneer Methodist missionary, Jason Lee, in the year 1836. (5) A State Temperance Union favoring legislative Prohibition had been formed in Oregon in 1873 and praying women marched against the saloons in Portland in 1874. (6) From 1906 to 1908, Clarence True Wilson was president of the Oregon State Anti-Saloon League. Under his leadership, the state Local Option Law was adopted and four-fifths of the state went dry within two years. He also saw the gambling establishments run out of business, all the saloons closed in Portland on Sundays, the nickel slot machines removed and destroyed, and statewide prohibition proposed in 1910. The proposal was defeated that year but passed four years later.

On Monday morning, June 6, 1910, Dr. Wilson addressed two hundred pastors at the Portland Ministerial Union on the subject "Why Oregon Is Going Dry":

> Oregon was founded by missionaries. The state of Oregon has more colleges in proportion to population than any other state. Oregon is a land of churches and schools. We could build up a consequential moral life from the Columbia River to the California line if it were not for a frowning fortress of hell firing into our lives all the time. While home and church and school are trying to make man better here, this great fort of the enemy is blazing away at our citadel and breaking up the four corner posts of civilization. These four posts are 1. honesty in business, 2. Sabbath observance, 3. purity of home life, and 4. temperance. The year 1910 will work an epoch in the contest regarding intemperance. The business of making drunkards out of Oregon's men is in

> ill repute, and we are hoping to end the stay right now. The liquor men are not engaged in a business like any other, and are entitled to no consideration based on the rights of a legitimate business...
>
> There are three classifications of enterprises. The first is business; the second charity; and the third is crime. Business is so much service or commodity and so much profit. Charity is all service without profit. Crime is all profit and no service. You may spend your money for fifty years over the bar and never get a thing better than a painted nose to show for your cash. The liquor traffic is an unfair competitor to every legitimate business, detrimental to their patrons as well as ruinous to the homes. If the $3,400,000 now spent in the 430 saloons of Portland were turned into the regular channels of trade every business in the city would increase. (7)

Dr. Wilson, still a young man when he came to Portland, took the city by storm much as he had other places. He believed that no church would prosper unless it addressed the matter of "public morals." He found gambling dens were flourishing in Portland, run mainly by persons of Asian descent. He said, regarding these vice merchants: "If we do not Christianize others, they will Paganize us." He found that there was a dark side to the restaurant business in Portland. Some of the restaurants had back rooms, boxes with locks on the doors. These were places where men could have "their way" and thus bring ruin to young girls.

Dr. Wilson supported the unwritten law that upheld protection of home and family. He urged "that sons be as carefully protected from the saloons as daughters from the brothel. The purpose of the law is to establish justice," he said in a Flag Day sermon calling for a "Stainless Flag Day." (8) A corrupt city council allowed vice to go unhindered. Dr. Wilson, with the help of other Protestant and Jewish leaders and the aid of the press and the platform, and an aroused public sentiment elected reform candidate, Dr. Harry Lane, as mayor.

As World War I loomed on the horizon, in Portland Dr. Wilson supported Oregon's Armory Measure. He saw the measure as being in the interest of young men, in the interest of national security, and in the interest of the welfare of the state.

Dr. Wilson longed for peace but he believed it possible only when there is force sufficient to insure it.

The statewide campaign for prohibition had all of Oregon listening. Debates between Dr. Wilson and Colonel E. Hofer, a Salem newspaper man, drew large crowds. "The drink traffic is a curse to any state," said Dr. Wilson. "Prohibition is a peril," claimed Hofer. "The Methodists are not in favor of increased beer tax. Revenue from the sale of intoxicants is blood money," said Dr. Wilson. "The liquor folks would welcome a tax as a life-saver for their doomed business," he continued. State license and tax would bring respectability to the liquor trade, believed Dr. Wilson. (9)

With all of this going on among the Portland ministers, a fellow pastor from Eugene, Oregon, became alarmed. Dr. I. D. Driver wrote of the goings-on in Portland: "My God, my God, who will defend the Christian religion? My ministerial brethren in Portland don't seem to preach about anything but the Sunday newspapers, Prohibition, and the slot machines." (10)

A more friendly critic was a lay member of Dr. Wilson's church who was pleased when Dr. Wilson announced a revival at Centenary Church. "Well, I followed you from Grace to Centenary Church, Dr. Wilson, and I've listened with pleasure to you preach on woman suffrage, about Sunday closing of saloons, against nickel-in-slot machines, and as to reforming the North End, but I'm glad, Dr. Wilson—downright glad— that you're going to do something religious at last!" (11)

The Idea of the move to Kansas was to preach prohibition from the bounds of the state which had made it a spectacular success.

— 4 —

Chicago and Topeka Years (1910-1916)

At age 38 Dr. Wilson made the-decision to devote all of his energy to the temperance reform movement. From their beginning in America in the late eighteenth century, Methodists had waged war on the liquor trade, though a permanent church committee on temperance was not established by the General Conference until 1888. In 1904 when the General Conference was held in Los Angeles, the Temperance Society of the Methodist Episcopal Church was formed. Bishop William Frazer McDowell was named president, and the Society was headquartered in Chicago. However, little action was forthcoming, as no direct way to secure funds was provided by the Conference. At the next General Conference in 1908, the Temperance Society was given a broader task and granted permission to request Sunday offerings. Bishop Robert Mclntyre was named president. Dr. W. A. Smith was named secretary and Alanzo E. Wilson, treasurer. Leaflets were published in 1908 through 1912. Aid was given to the dry campaign in Oklahoma. But the work idled along.

The breakthrough came in May 1910. The Society decided to elect two clergy to devote full time to temperance reform. Clarence True Wilson was appointed field secretary and Dr. Alfred Smith, assistant secretary. They began work without an office, desk, or a cent of regular income and no guarantee of salary or expenses. The Temperance Society was a paper organization only. Dr. Wilson opened an office in the Methodist Book Concern Building in Chicago. He said later the office was little more than a broom closet.

Deets Pickett, who was later to become the research secretary for the Board of Temperance, first met Dr. Wilson in Chicago. Pickett wrote about their first meeting:

> I think it was in 1910 when I was in Chicago doing editorial work that I first met Dr. Clarence True Wilson. It was a case of friendship at first sight. Our minds seemed to be headed in the same direction in regard to almost all public questions. In a vague way, I knew that he was doing "temperance" work, but that he was not with the Anti-Saloon League, and I became more and more curious as to just what his connection was.
>
> "Who is Dr. Wilson, anyway," I asked a friend, "and who is behind him?"
>
> "Well," he replied, "theoretically, the Methodist Church is behind him, but practically he is just behind himself. He was a popular pastor in a big city church out West, but gave it up to become General Secretary of the Temperance Society of the Methodist Episcopal Church. The Society is really nothing but

a name; it has no support and no headquarters. Dr. Wilson is speaking almost constantly, selling books to pay his expenses from place to place, and amuses himself by circulating thousands of leaflets on the streets in between times. He publishes quite a good many leaflets, and when he gets an order, his wife wraps them up and ships them out. I believe they have desk room in somebody else's office down the street."

One day, after I had become still better acquainted with the Doctor, I said:

"Dr. Wilson, why should a man with your personality and ability waste time holding a position which is held in such light esteem by the Methodist Church that it does not even carry a salary or an office or an expense account? Do you think it is treating your wife fairly to spend what little money you have saved supporting her and yourself while you are working night and day doing work without compensation?"

I never shall forget his reply. We were standing in an office at the corner of LaSalle and Washington Streets, Chicago. He said, "Come over to the window a moment." I did so. And he pointed to the city streets. "Mr. Pickett," he said, "the Methodist Church has been at war with the liquor traffic since it got out of the cradle; isn't that so? John Wesley said: 'The liquor traffic drives His Majesty's subjects to hell like sheep,' and the General Conference has said: 'It can never be legalized without sin,' and 'License high or low is vicious in principle and powerless as a remedy.' You and I know that the Church has gotten nowhere in its war on the liquor traffic. They obey no law made for their regulation. They have rooms for prostitution upstairs, and rooms for gambling behind. They sell to minors and they sell on Sunday. They pay graft and there are plenty of takers. Oh, I know that we have a few prohibition States. There is faithful old Maine, still standing by its law, and the entire liquor traffic of the Nation closely organized for offensive effort, does everything possible to break down the local laws of Maine and Kansas and North Dakota. Under the protection of Interstate Commerce the liquor traffic grows more arrogant, more corrupt, and more powerful ev-ery day. Isn't that so?

"Now," he said, "I will tell you the reason. When a speaker goes to town to make a Prohibition address, he goes straight to the nearest church, does he not? When a Prohibition paper is put into the mails, it is addressed to somebody who is sufficiently interested in Prohibition to have made a contribution to the cause. That is all very commendable work, but it will never win this fight. We will have to make speeches to people who are not convinced and we will have to sow the land knee deep in Prohibition literature, reaching the people who do not particularly want to read it. We must go out into the highways and byways and compel

> them to come. This is a missionary job, and when the Church of Christ awakes to that fact, we will have the liquor traffic on the run. I am preaching that principle to the Methodist Church; there are hundreds of thousands of Methodists who already agree with me, and I have faith that Methodism will yet tackle this job on a missionary basis." (1)

From the beginning Dr. Wilson did not spend a great amount of time at his Chicago office. After all, he was field secretary and much of his time was spent in the field. He truly was a "traveling elder" of the Methodist Episcopal Church. An early speaking event was the Temperance Field Day November 19, 1911, in Washington, Pennsylvania. In a speech titled "A World Vision of the Temperance Reform," Dr. Wilson spoke of the status of temperance reform in fifty countries. He emphasized the "Cathmeapal" movement started in Ireland in 1908, through which three million persons had pledged to be total abstainers. While in Washington, Pennsylvania, he spoke three times that day to large crowds at churches in the morning and evening and at the Young Men's Christian Association gym in the afternoon.

He asked, "Is the beer industry a business or a crime?" He said businesses deal in necessities of life. They provide services on a small margin of profit. They offer credit to those who need services but are short on cash. The beer industry provides no necessities of life, operates on a large margin of profit, and does not give credit, thus robbing the poor of cash that could go to buy necessities. He quoted his favorite text, going back to his first temperance talk as a boy of sixteen, "Wherever you find it, the liquor traffic is the blood-sucking leech among all the business industries of the community." These words he had first heard from the lips of his father.

> "The next step of Christian civilization is to put down the whole liquor traffic. The court of New York State, twenty years ago declared that gambling is not a business but a crime. When you get something for nothing you are a thief. When you get nothing for something you are a fool. The saloon also is in this same class. It is a crime not a business. It takes logs for a saw mill. It takes boys to run a saloon. The license system is lame in logic and a failure in practice," he said. (2)

Another major step was taken at the 1912 General Conference. The Temperance Society became the Board of Temperance and the office was moved to Topeka, Kansas. The General Conference apportioned $50,000 for the work of the board. That same year the General Conference passed strong resolutions condemning the Taft Administration for use of the State Department in promoting the beer-makers' sales in foreign nations, and in sustaining James Wilson as Secretary of the Department of Agriculture after his participation in the Brewers' Congress. The General Conference endorsed the Woman's Christian Temperance Union, Anti-Saloon League, and other movements for overthrow of the liquor traffic.

The idea of the move to Kansas was to preach prohibition from the bounds of the state which had made it a spectacular success. In that year, Deets Pickett, who had known Dr. Wilson in Chicago, was invited to join the staff. When he arrived in Topeka, Miss Bates, the office secretary, met Pickett at the office. "Where is Dr. Wilson?" asked Pickett. "Dr. Wilson is on a speaking campaign in the West. Mr. J. C. McDowell of Pittsburgh has given him a Reo automobile, and his little daughter is driving it. He is speaking places which cannot be reached by railroad," she told him.

The "Prohibition Water Wagon," as Dr. Wilson called it, was making history on that trip. The cornet would blow, and the gospel of prohibition would be expounded. Preaching in front of a factory was common. He spoke with no police protection, yet no harm came to him. Nearly all those who heard him speak promised to vote dry. Often the speaking was done from the top of a beer keg. One time, when a man poked fun at the preacher for standing on a keg, Dr. Wilson replied, "I see by your shape that you have swallowed yours." On another occasion, one of the enemy in the crowed hissed. "Ah," said the Doctor, "there is another red nose in cold water. I heard it sizzle." There was no more hissing.

Although Oregon defeated prohibition in 1910, Dr. Wilson traveled there in 1912 and again in 1914 to help in the campaign for state prohibition. Before leaving Oregon in 1910, Dr. Wilson had debated Colonel E. Hofer, a Salem newspaper man who opposed prohibition. They were again on the debate platform together in 1912 and 1914. In all, fifty-four debates were held at nearly every county fair and

Chautauqua in the state as well as in the big city opera houses. It has been said that these debates drew the greatest audiences that had ever been drawn by any political meetings within the borders of the state. These debates helped put the state of Oregon in the dry column.

Dr. Wilson saw a great victory for his efforts during the year 1914 in Oregon. The state voted for statewide prohibition November 3, 1914, by a wide margin. The law did not take effect until January 1, 1916. By the end of the first year, Dr. Wilson reported the positive results. Penitentiary admissions had decreased by 42 percent. The Multnomah County (which includes Portland) poor farm decreased admissions by 44 percent. Fires were cut by 50 percent. Thirty-five police placements were dropped, while the population increased by 25 percent. Christmas 1916 found 67 prisoners housed, while there had been 157 on Christmas of 1915. The consumption of alcoholic beverage was reduced by 88 percent. (3)

One of the most unusual developments of this period, while the Board of Temperance was located in Topeka, was the Flying Squadron Campaign of 1914-1915 to promote the cause of prohibition. The Flying Squadron Foundation was headquartered in Indianapolis, Indiana. The campaign, sponsored by the Foundation, began September 30, 1914, in Peoria, Illinois, and ended June 6, 1915, in Atlantic City, New Jersey. In 235 days, speaking teams visited 255 cities. They embraced every capital city, every large city, and every educational center in the United States. These speakers resolved in their hearts that the American people should hear their message, without regard to the cost to the speakers in time, effort, or money.

Three groups of speakers made possible visits to three cities on the same day. Two meetings were held each day, one in the afternoon and the other in the evening. These speakers were able to reach a million people. The nation became a great university, whose "students" were given a required course on the dangers of the liquor traffic. These speakers hit straight from the shoulders. The talks were delivered by "professors" who were going somewhere and knew why and how they were going. They came to the task with the spirit of love and devotion. The visit of the Squadron was equal to a religious revival in moral force and power. All were aflame with a consuming passion for the destruction of the saloon. The liquor traffic is weaker and all righteous forces are stronger since these addresses were delivered.

Among these speakers was Dr. Clarence True Wilson. Here are some of the thoughts he shared on that historic barnstorming tour of America. His talks came under the general heading of "Cracked Chestnuts." He would tackle a few of the objections to prohibition progress as cracking a few chestnuts "to let some of the dark out."

> "Saloon keeping is a legitimate business!"
>
> "[To this his response was] Christian civilization is supported by four pillars. 1. Integrity in Business. Against this pillar is gambling mania. 2. Sabbath observance. Against this is Sunday desecration. 3. Purity of home life. Against this is license for the

places of shame (prostitution), and 4. Sobriety of the people. Against this is a stream of drunkenness.

"The saloon is not a business but a crime. It takes three classes of human activity. There are business, charity, and crime. The saloon offers nothing but a red nose. You say the liquor business helps by paying taxes. Not so, you can not get water from a sponge."

"Why stir everybody up on the temperance question?"

"[His answer was] Because the license system is eternally wrong. Unsettled moral problems have no mercy on the peace of the nation. Agitation is better than stagnation. For this he gave an example of a frog that falls in a pail of cream. Instead of giving up for dead it stirred up the cream until it turned into butter and climbed out of the mess. Two ministers go to the same community. One has a passion for home and country. He represents the vicious minority that is always active for reform. The other is the righteous majority that is closed or asleep.

"A dozen righteous men can bring in a reign of righteousness anywhere. Law enforcement is easy when you have the man. When Carrie Nation took her ax to the saloon, every joint keeper in Kansas found that one woman was too much for them."

"But isn't this sentiment a mere spasm?"

"[To this Wilson responded with a list of causes that contribute to the effects we now see.] For thirty years there has been the influence of the Quarterly Temperance Lessons. For twenty years there has been the influence of instruction in the public schools on the harmful effects of alcoholic drink. There have been other causes as well. The insurance companies that will not insure the drunk, the railway corporations and the secret societies that reject the drinker, there has been the voice of the church, the decisions of the courts, the police records, all united to point out the saloon as the people's Supreme Foe. We all stand together when the time comes to close in on the liquor traffic.

"When a minister, a teacher or a social worker goes into a community the one institution that blocks his (or her) work and destroys what the teacher is trying to build up is the saloon. We are not going to vote much longer for our worst rival. We have other plans for our young people than feeding them to the saloon."

"Temptation must needs come."

"[To this he replied] As if we had to side with the devil in order to make the Lord a true prophet. Prohibition is not to make men moral but to stop a traffic that injures people.

This argument shows disrespect to the devil. It implies that he is not equal to the task. Temptation is the devil's job, not ours."

"You can't make men moral by compulsory legislation."

"[The reply] Prohibition is not an attempt to make men moral. Criminal law is enacted to protect the community against wrongdoing. The saloon breeds crime against the person, against public order, against life itself. We ought to stop making men immoral by law. Men may get liquor if they hunt it, but we ought to stop the saloon from hunting men."

"One out of ten makes a fool by drinking, why deprive the other nine the pleasure of drink?"

"The drinker makes a wild beast of himself and he is liable to make a corpse of somebody else. If one coat that was sold brings harm we get rid of the coats. If one ice cream brought harm we would get rid of the ice cream. If liquor were an entirely new thing, we would not allow it. There need be no law against drunkenness if a person is living apart, but if he is going to live in society, there can be no true liberty but in steadfast obedience to right law."

"It is contrary to Liberty to dictate what a man shall eat or drink."

"Here is a double misconception [says Wilson]. The first is as to the nature of personal rights and the other as to the purpose of prohibition. Liberty has to do with one's own person, but when others are affected, my right stops! Barter requires social organization. There is a requirement for protection of civil laws. The right to control a public traffic is a civil right."

"It is a bad thing to have laws that are not en-forced."

"Yes, but a worse thing to have are laws which decent people cannot respect. One who sells liquor should be called a skunk. That is the beast that dispenses strong liquor without a license!"

"Prohibition don't prohibit."

"The logic is as bad as the grammar. Prohibition has worked to outlaw dueling, slavery, and polygamy. It works on election day and on Sunday. The same legal system could make it work on every other day."

"The brewers have agreed to reform!"

"Well, in Oregon this was the promise. When the election was over, all these pre-election promises, like some New Year's resolution, folded their tents like the Arabs and silently stole away. The liquor trade will never be reformed so long as alcohol dwells in whiskey. The only way to reform the trade is to turn every saloon into a store."

"A half loaf is better than no bread."

"That depends, is the half loaf poisoned? The half loaf answer reduces the number of saloons. There is no record that it has reduced the evils of drink. The saloons that are left do about twice as much business."

"Why not work for enforcement?" "The reason being that saloons must continually be watched. The laws can be enforced only through the public officials. The best .way to reform a saloon is to close it up and then start

> some other business there. You say work to improve the saloon? We are not in the liquor business. Crime should be prohibited; wrong cannot be right."
>
> "But of two evils you must choose the least."
>
> "Of two evils there is no choice for me. One is rotten, the other spoiled. I will wait till the hen lays fresh eggs. The license system is not a restriction of a prohibition, but a legal permission to do a wrong act. The license system provides respectability to an evil and provides revenue from an evil source." (4)

These were the fighting words of Dr. Wilson as he joined with the Flying Squadron to educate America regarding the drink problem during the campaign of 1914-1915.

In addition to public speeches, Dr. Wilson published a popular newsletter. The first issue of *The Voice* of the Temperance Society of the Methodist Episcopal Church came out in March 1914. The front page of the four-page newsletter announced: "This quarterly is circulated exclusively among the pastors of the Methodist Church, to furnish them with brief, current temperance matter for their use." In the second year of printing, *The Voice* became a monthly publication. *The Voice* informed pastors that the harm of alcohol is not a modern discovery.

There are ancient warnings against alcoholic drink. Do not suppose the present remarkable interest in prohibition will automatically convert itself into victory. Victory will come when churches deserve it.

> The question of prohibition is federal in its scope. The constitution is "the people's law." Once enshrined ... there will not be the remotest chance to remove it. We hear lots of reaction from the wet side but remember a frisky colt stops short of action. (5)

During January and February 1914 *The Voice* reported there were four meetings per day in the western states of Oregon, Montana, and California in the statewide campaigns for prohibition. The field details were managed by staff member Harry G. McCain. The sixty-day campaign involved an auto trip to remote cities of the West. A mid-March trip was conducted in eastern states. (6)

The Voice encouraged working with the Anti-Saloon League. "The two oars of legislation (the Anti-Saloon League) and education (the Temperance Societies) must pull together or we will go around in circles with little progress." The March 1, 1914, issue reported:

> More than half of the United States was then covered by some form of prohibition. The new Webb-Kenyon interstate bill has proven most valuable. There is, however, great danger from brewers' propaganda among the foreign-born in our great cities. Foreigners' higher drink consumption is located in the license centers of the large eastern cities. There is large increase for beer trade among fami-

> lies. Women and children are drinking beer in their homes. Twenty percent of beer output is in bottles. There is an increase in icebox trade. While the brewers claim to promote moderation, the 1200 persons attending the Brewers' Congress drank 9000 bottles of beer. (7)

These were some of the bits of information provided the reader in the first issues of *The Voice.*

Nursery tales were reconstructed to teach temperance lessons to children. Alcohol outside the body is a good friend; alcohol inside the body is poison. Sunday School programs were developed with new songs from the Temperance Society. William A. Quayle, later to become a Methodist Episcopal Bishop, was very much delighted with *The Voice.* He said, "It is the sort of plunder that will make good thunder for temperance workers." (8)

By moving to the nation's capital, the Board of Temperance became like a city set on a hill.

— 5 —

Move to Washington and Prohibition Victory (1916-1920)

In the summer of 1916, Dr. Wilson made the move to Washington. The name of the agency was changed from the Board of Temperance to the Board of Temperance, Prohibition, and Public Morals. It was from Washington, "the connection center of the union," that the final battle for national Prohibition was to move on to victory.

Before leaving Topeka, Dr. Wilson received the following letter from Arthur Capper, governor of Kansas, dated June 5, 1916.

Dear Doctor Wilson:

I see by the papers that you are soon to take the temperance headquarters of the Methodist Church to Washington. We are sorry to have you leave Topeka, but I can see how you can probably work to better advantage with headquarters at Washington. I am very much interested in your work and I hope you will let me know when I can be of any service to you.

I believe national Prohibition is the most important issue before the people of this country today. I am confident we are to have national Prohibition much sooner than we expected. (1)

Dr. Wilson may have been one of the nation's first cross- continent commuters, his new office address being 204 Pennsylvania Avenue, S.E., in a historic building that once housed the Supreme Court when the Capitol burned in 1812. His home address remained at the farm near Gresham, Oregon, about fifteen miles from Portland's city center. One wonders how the supervision of the move to Washington was completed, for Dr. Wilson was still very much a "field secretary."

During the summer of 1916 Wilson left Washington for Montana and the Pacific coast in the ever-faithful six-cylinder Reo automobile. In 1916 the Reo was the latest in technological advances. The Reo had been presented to the Methodist Board of Temperance by J. C. McDowell of Pittsburgh. Wilson called it the "water-wagon." The goal of this campaign was to turn the tide in several western states in favor of national Prohibition.

The October 1916 issue of The Voice reported on the campaign of the summer of 1916:

Did you ever see a torpedo boat destroyer? Here it comes, menacing smoke pouring from its funnels, rocking, swaying, and spitting flame from its guns. There is nothing indecisive about it.

That is Clarence True Wilson on the platform. There is roll and sway and salt flavor to his words, there is menacing logic in every paragraph, there is rhetoric foaming before his advance, but standing out above all in the picture are the staccato facts which precede with crackling snap the thud of the target. Always, his speech has the purposeful direction, the speed and the efficiency, of a torpedo boat destroyer.

In one little city a half drunken man and a saloon keeper disturbed the meeting. Dr. Wilson called the drunken man forward to present his side. His drunken plea was wonderfully effective for prohibition. When the crowd started to leave the Doctor stopped them, saying, "I have another 'wet orator to introduce," and pointed to a man who had interrupted with insulting remarks. In a second nothing but the man's coat-tails were visible. In one town a meeting was held on the saloon porch. In several, drunken men attempted to break up the meetings. In some places the police were enlisted by the wets but without avail. In San Francisco the Water-wagoners were warned that the feeling was so tense as to make it dangerous to hold meetings, but hundreds listened with profound attention. Six thou-sand laboring men surrounded the speakers near the gates of an ironworks, and although it was alleged that they would tear the car into pieces, they listened respectfully.

The deviltry of this country is done by the idle rich and the idle poor, not by the workers of any class, said Dr. Wilson. (2)

The Voice appealed to the Methodists to aid in the advance toward national Prohibition. It was believed that the December 1916 session of Congress would offer unprecedented opportunity for Methodists to seize two mighty reforms for God and America.

By moving to the nation's capital, the Board of Temperance became like a city set upon a hill. The Library of Congress provided unlimited resources that greatly strengthened the research work of the Society. News sources, such as the legislative offices of the Anti-Saloon League and International Reform Bureau and the numerous news correspondence offices, added to an already large list of sources available to the Board of Temperance, putting the board in an unrivaled position as a distributor of Prohibition news and arguments. (3)

A strategy of the Board was to get all 18,000 Methodist pastors to concentrate their efforts upon winning the press.

> By united action we can emancipate the daily newspapers of the country from the domination of liquor advertisements and, indeed, we may be able to drive liquor advertising from the mails entirely. (4)

The goal of the Board of Temperance, Prohibition, and Public Morals was to move in where the need was imperative. It was not the desire of the Board to duplicate any work that was already being done by any other temperance reform organization. Among the projects needing attention were the work among the immigrant population and the need for increased educational efforts among the African-American people, who had received little or no education regarding alcohol. The Board also campaigned to get major newspapers to refuse liquor advertisements. The Board was also involved in the re-election campaigns of several Congressmen, including Representative Randall of California, who was a strong supporter of the national Prohibition movement. (5)

The move to Washington put Dr. Wilson in touch not only with Congressional leaders, but also with the President and the cabinet. On December 6, 1916, Dr. Wilson received an invitation to meet with President Woodrow Wilson at the White House at 3 p.m., December 14th. This visit was symbolic of the high-water mark of Methodism's influence on public life in the pre-Prohibition Era. (6)

A *Cyclopedia of Temperance* written by Dr. Wilson and Pickett in 1917 provided a wealth of resources on temperance history and efforts of the day for statewide and national prohibition. In the Cyclopedia were such bits of information as reporting of a 1915 Alabama law prohibiting liquor advertisement in newspapers in that state. Regarding advertisements of alcohol the Cyclopedia said: 'The purpose of advertising and solicitation is to cause demand where demand did not previously exist." (7) There was in the Cyclopedia an article on the effects of alcohol on the body. Statistics were given on the 1916 per capita consumption of liquors, as well as the cost to the nation's economy and the crime rate related to drinking of alcohol. A January 1, 1917, listing of all newspapers in the country that had agreed to exclude all liquor advertising was also included. There was in the 1917 edition a listing of anti-Prohibition arguments and the board's response to each argument with a statement of the benefits of Prohibition. An article reported problems related to drinking in the army and a report was given regarding a movement among soldiers for abstinence. The reader was educated regarding the term "Blind Pigs" and other names given to the unlicensed establishments that sold liquor. The public was informed regarding the work of the Board of Temperance, Prohibition, and Public Morals. The term "bone dry" was explained to the reader and states that had bone dry laws were listed.

Another article discussed the so-called "reform" proposed by the beer brewers of the nation. The possible offer of compensation to liquor dealers if national Prohibition became law was the subject of yet another article. The case for a constitutional Prohibition amendment was skillfully set forth by the authors. This pocket book of temperance reform information was made available to every pastor in the Methodist Episcopal Church in order to arm the clergy with an arsenal to use in agitation for national Prohibition. The pastors were expected to pass on this valuable information, based on research by the Board, to the press in their communities, as well as influence their legislators to support temperance reform and national Prohibition.

The 1917 *Yearbook of Churches and Agencie*s outlined the work of the Methodist Board of Temperance, Prohibition and Public Morals: "A field force is maintained, work is carried on in Sunday Schools and Epworth Leagues and among colored people, as well as extensive research and publicity." (8)

In 1918, a new six-cylinder Reo seven-passenger

car was purchased by the Board to replace the 1912 car. This new car was as "swift as a bird on the mountains," it was reported, and Dr. Wilson was not long in waiting to sweep the country once again in this new automobile. (9)

As World War I began to unfold in Europe and the numbers of soldiers in readiness in the United States were on the increase, the Board became increasingly concerned regarding cigarette smoking, as well as drinking, among the soldiers. Providing free cigarettes for soldiers was viewed as an assault on the American flag, a view that may well have been a full fifty years in advance of its time.

The increasing possibility of United States involvement in the war and the "Red Scare" of 1919-1920 increased support for Prohibition and immigration restriction. Distrust of German-American brewers eased passage of the Eighteenth Amendment and the Volstead Act, which provided for enforcement of the Amendment. (10)

Dr. Wilson and The Voice sounded the alarm that German Jews had taken control of the liquor traffic as well as control of moving pictures, that were, in his view, along with stage productions, reflecting increasingly that kind of "vulgar smut" that was popular in the European theater. Also of concern was the "dirty picture" mail order trade coming out of California. He also spoke out against the dismissal of all restraints of decency across the border in Tijuana, Mexico. (11)

The Board, in making appeal for financial support for its work for public morality and decency, proclaimed, "Every dollar goes into actual net accomplishment. The Board of Temperance pays dividends in fat golden results. The occasion is piled high with difficulties and we must rise to the occasion." (12)

Admiration was high for Dr. Wilson during these pre-Prohibition years of 1916 to 1920. "What a whirlwind of a man is Dr. Clarence True Wilson. What a fighter, a strategist, a campaigner, an indefatigable worker. What an inspirational message he gave us as he reviewed the history of the Prohibition success, and briefly outlined the future. How John Barleycorn must hate him, but how we all love him. It was fitting climax to a week of climaxes." (13)

His address to the Methodist Episcopal General Conference May 1, 1920, in Des Moines, Iowa, entitled "Methodism and Temperance Reform," stands at the very pinnacle of his influence in the life of the church and nation.

This building is representative not only of some chief activities of one of the great religious denominations of the nation but also an architectural contribution to our Capital City, already noted as the most beautiful in the world.

— 6 —

The Story of the Methodist Building

The construction of The Methodist Building was a truly amazing accomplishment. For over eighty years it has been the headquarters of Methodist's social action agencies. It is somewhat of a miracle that Dr. Clarence True Wilson was able to locate prime District of Columbia property at 100 Maryland Avenue, facing the east side of the Capitol Building. The property belonged to a group of squabbling heirs. Wilson patiently tracked down and bought out each of them, paying $27,500 for the vacant lot. On that property for a mere million dollars was built an elegant and utilitarian building in the year 1923. The building was dedicated with great fanfare, January 16, 1924.

When the building was completed it housed the Board of Temperance, Prohibition and Public Morals of The Methodist Episcopal Church. On the top three floors were apartments, many rented to Congressmen. The profits from the rentals were dedicated to the work of the agency.

The building was designed and engineered by the Ballinger Company, Architects and Engineers, Philadelphia and New York, and stands as a monument to the leadership and stubborn determination, not only of Dr. Wilson but his wife Maude as well. The style of the building is Italian Renaissance. The V shape, five stories and basement were determined by zoning laws of the day. The apartments were designed to appeal to a very desirable class of tenants. According to a promotional brochure at the time: "This building is representative not only of some chief activities of one of the great religious denominations of the nation but also an architectural contribution to our Capital City, already noted as the most beautiful in the world." (1)

Perhaps more attention needs to be paid to the important role played by Maude Wilson as "Secretary of the Methodist Building." Her duties were that of keeping the building in good repair, purchasing and arranging furniture in the lobbies, furnishing apartments, supervising the staff, finding applicants for residence, and looking into their fitness for living in the apartments. In the late 1920's rents for the seventy apartments ranged from $45 to $150 per month.

Mrs. Wilson began as an unpaid secretary to her husband from the very beginning of their work for the temperance cause in 1910. Maude Wilson made arrangements for his travels. She made out all expense accounts and attended to all of the detail work which her husband's constant traveling made impossible for him to do. In 1933 she reported to the board that they had twenty-three years earlier left the pastorate with furnished parsonage and an adequate salary to begin this work with no office and for eighteen months without income. They used up all of their life savings, having to borrow on a life insurance policy in order for their daughters to go to college. (2)

Each year Mrs. Wilson gave a report to the board regarding income from the apartments and gifts that had been given to support the work of the board. In 1926 she asked for a piano for the conference room and fifty hymnals and a fine old grandfather clock for the vestibule. Each year she kept her request for the clock until she finally got it. (3)

In her 1927 report she recommended that funds be raised to buy the property next to the building for an annex, providing space for more apartments thus more revenue to fund the work of the agency. It was hoped to have the annex completed by 1929, the Tenth Anniversary of the adoption of the Prohibition Amendment. (4)

An important part of the building was the Bishop Matthew Simpson Memorial Chapel. A gift of $25,000 provided furnishing of the chapel and an endowment for an annual lectureship. The Chapel was dedicated January 16th, 1929. By December of 1930 the Annex was still not a reality. The adjoining property was purchased as a cost of $74,000. A gift of $40,000 was applied of the debt. It was necessary to mortgage all properties in order to borrow $500,000 for the new structure. This turned out to be a blessing. With one less floor there was a savings of $100,000. (5)

At first the board wanted to call the new building "The Congressional" but it was later decided not to emphasize either the relations to church or state, so it was simply designate "110 Maryland Avenue, N.E." It seemed that it was built in times out of joint.

There were too many units being built in the city. Other apartment owners would take tenants away promising apartments that had rented for $275 for as low as $125 if they would move. Mrs. Wilson was fearful she would have to report to the board a building only half full, yet when it came time for the board meeting she was able to report seventy out of the seventy-five units in the Annex full and all but one in the main building. (6)

The Annex was built by Charles H. Tompkins Company. Mrs. Wilson reported the company built well and saved the agency a lot of money. The Tompkins Company was paid $333,000, but provided a refund of $15,000 to take care of the stone front required by the government. The actual cost to the agency was $315,000. (7)

During this time Dr. Wilson became gravely ill and was in the hospital so Mr. Wilson had to make many decisions by herself. Also, in 1933 they faced the disappointment of the repeal of Prohibition, a cause to which they had devoted so much energy. These were also the years of the Great Depression. As a result, many great buildings of the city had gone into receiver's hands, unable even to pay interest or insurance. What a marvelous gift The Methodist Building proved to be thanks to the efforts of Dr. and Mrs. Wilson. The building is now The United Methodist Building and houses among other agencies The board of Church and Society of the United Methodist Church.

Symbolic of the social welfare ministry of Dr. Wilson and the Board of Temperance was the Pay-Day sculpture created by a French artist and displayed on the main floor of the building. The sculpture is a figure of a woman with a child clutching her mother's skirt, looking down at a fallen man, in whose hand is the neck of a broken bottle. The charge was being made that Methodists simply wanted to squash pleasure everywhere. The symbolism of the *Pay-Day* sculpture was the perfect retort, because it dramatized how drink made so much of humankind unhappy. In a way, *Pay-Da*y says it all in summing up the message of Dr. Wilson's ministry.

Following World War I, both church leaders and politicians were divided over the wisdom of the prohibition law.

— 7 —

Prohibition Years (1920-1933)

From Triumph to Demise

The Eighteenth Amendment was adopted by Congress and sent to the states for ratification December 18, 1917. Ratified by thirty-six states by January 16, 1919, Prohibition became law January 16, 1920. It seemed the battle had been won. However, this was not the case. Passage of the Eighteenth Amendment was simply the battle cry to action for enforcement and respect for the law. Following World War I, both church leaders and politicians were divided over the wisdom of the Prohibition law. A growing split within Protestantism turned into a chasm. Democrats were virtually disabled by divisions over Prohibition. Support for Prohibition was not inherently nativist. Some foreign-born Catholics joined in the movement. (1)

Dr. Wilson, popular with church leaders in America who backed the Prohibition cause, soon gained international acclaim following the Prohibition victory in America. He was elected a delegate to the fifth ecumenical Methodist Conference in London and addressed the conference September 15, 1921, on "The Practicability of the Christian Ideals." He told the delegation:

> The most destructive heresy of our times is the mistrust as to whether the Christian ideals are practicable. In the view of John Wesley the highest New Testament standards are attainable by the humblest believer. The goal of the Methodist movement was to eliminate personal vices among converts. Wesley was a Prohibitionist 150 years ahead of his time. Wesley the greatest evangelist was the most farseeing of social reformers. Religion and ethics are not separate. Religion is morality as related to God. Morality is religion in relation to man. Wesley viewed the liquor trade as enemy of church and home. The liquor traffic could never be legalized without sin. Tax on liquor is no proper source of revenue.
>
> Rejoice that Prohibition has come to America. America is pointing the way for other nations. Prohibition is here to stay. Politicians no longer kneel before it (the liquor industry) for political patronage. It is now possible to preach the gospel to a sober people. Do not be deceived by the well financed propaganda of the liquor industry. Truth comes from law-abiding citizens. Prohibition enforcement is not perfect in America, but we are making the greatest moral epoch of the Christian centuries. The church is leading the reform. Let us not compromise with sin. Praise God who

heals the drunkard. (2)

On May 5, 1923, Dr. Wilson was invited to speak at the 143rd anniversary services at Barratt's Chapel near Dover, Delaware. The chapel is one of the oldest churches in America. Later that summer Dr. Wilson made the "Hall of Famous Preachers and Lecturers" by being invited to speak at the Ocean Grove Summer School and Camp Meeting in New Jersey. Preaching services at Ocean Grove sometimes drew crowds of 8000 to 9000 persons. The brochure for the 1923 season gives a glimpse of Methodism in the nineteen-twenties, and the men (only two women featured) who provided leadership.

Also in July 1923, while Dr. Wilson was vacationing in Oregon, he was invited to give four addresses at a camp meeting in Cottage Grove. One of the addresses was his talk on "The Holy Spirit." When he gave the same address at the Metropolitan Church in Washington, D.C., one reporter wrote: "The greatest address it has ever been my privilege to hear on the subject." (3) Thursday, October 11, 1923, Dr. Wilson spoke at the Founders' Day Celebration of Princess Anne Academy, Eastern Branch of the University of Maryland. His topic "My Father as I Knew Him." September 25, 1921, Dr. Wilson addressed the Southern California Annual Conference of the Methodist Episcopal Church. "Get into politics," Dr. Wilson exhorted the church leaders. Speaking under the heading "Religion, Morality, and Politics," Dr. Wilson gave a graphic exposition of the triumph of Prohibition. He imbued the pastors of 250 southern California churches with the conviction that upon them rested the responsibility of inculcating the principles of good government into the younger generation, while leading the old into battle on the right side of the political arena.

> "Get into politics!" was the tenor of his exhortation. "If the forces of God—the saints—can't present as strong a lineup, and wield as much influence as the forces of evil—the devils—there can't be much doubt as to the outcome. Dr. Wilson had small praise for persons who pretended to be devout Methodists, and yet did not with due zeal and diligence exercise their power of the franchise "He is no Christian!" Dr. Wilson decried the policy of separating the church from the state. "The fundamentals of American government rest upon the church. The principles of the Constitution are drawn from the laws of Moses, and now the Bible has been crowded out of the public schools in all but four states!"
>
> Dr. Wilson crisply scored the pastor who fails to lead an active political campaign for better government and for the best men to head that government.
>
> The speaking platform can never lead in the great movement for civic reform. It is too intermittent. The public press cannot lead the movement. It is run for cash, not for conscience. No force motivated by a desire for dollars can effect the reform. The stage cannot lead the movement. In three thousand years the stage has shown no evidence of fighting for

> the slightest moral betterment. Who can lead? The preachers. We modern preachers are not priests. Jesus Christ was the last priest. We are prophets, the prophets of God, who plunge into every great battle, who mix into everything. We must be moral leaders, the spiritual power for righteousness.
>
> It was the church militant, that by preaching the gospel had driven piracy from the seas, killed the slave trade, eliminated dueling, polygamy, lotteries, the liquor traffic—and prize-fighting in all the civilized states. "We've killed the liquor traffic in America!" he said. "But we're not through. In five or ten years the map of Europe will be speckled. In a few years more all Europe will be as white as the United States. Prohibition will be international!"
>
> Dr. Wilson thundered that Prohibition in America is an unequivocal success, and that the Volstead Act is as firmly entrenched as Gibraltar in the foundation of government. (4)

The theme of United States ideals inspired by the Bible was put forth by Dr. Wilson in an address at the Churchmen's Luncheon at the City Club in Washington, D.C., December 6, 1924. Dr. Wilson declared that the probable inspiration for the American form of government was first found in the Bible. He told the group assembled that an insistent demand should be made for the return of the Bible into every public school in the country.

From Holland to ancient Rome many of the older governments of Europe have sometime or another claimed to have been the inspiration for the American Republic. It was from the Holy Bible that the founders of this country took their ideal. Dr. Wilson cited a remarkable parallel between the Constitution of the United States and Constitution of ancient Israel.

For five hundred twenty years Israel had no king. The ancient Hebrew Constitution and the Constitution of the United States were the only documents of their kind ever submitted to the people for ratification. Rome never knew the time when there was even a semblance of equality in its government.

When the Hebrews cried for a king their leaders told them that God was their King. And when a committee of colonists from Baltimore, Philadelphia, and New York went to George Washington, at Mount Vernon, and told him the country was breaking up like a rope of sand, that he must come forward and be the King, he picked up the Holy Bible and recited those very words to the delegation.

> It is a national shame that the Book from which the forefathers took their inspiration of a true republic— the Government that is now America—should be crowded out of the schools. (5)

The success of Prohibition was due not alone to the influence of the church but to the support of business and industrial leaders. Henry Ford was a strong advocate for Prohibition. He saw the law as good for business. His orders were that no worker could smell of liquor and that no worker in the Ford Motor plants could have any liquor in his home. He viewed the Eighteenth Amendment as simply a part of the law of the land. In his view you simply could not weaken one law without weakening all law. (6)

An article by Dr. Wilson appeared in *The Adult Bible Class Monthly*, August 1927, entitled "Our Unfinished Task." In the article Dr. Wilson claims:

> Prohibition has not yet had a fair chance. To date no one has been appointed to head up enforcement who was a friend of Prohibition. No reform ever makes headway which allows itself to be put on the defensive. We need as a nation a new personal stand of respect for law. (He outlined six things that must be done to enforce Prohibition.)
>
> 1. We should punish the buyer as well as the seller of poisoned bootleg liquor;
> 2. We should make the first offense involve a prison sentence;
> 3. We must deport aliens who are convicted of violating our law;
> 4. Judges must padlock offending places;
> 5. We must cease depending on Uncle Sam to do for us what as States we can do for ourselves; and
> 6. We must elect men to office who are in hearty sympathy with the law.
>
> Prohibition has been tried and found wanting, said a critic... but the truth is, prohibition was found difficult and therefore not tried. To live Christian ideals in a world like this is not

> the pastime of an hour but a manly, self-sacrificing, cross-bearing work of a lifetime... if we make good on this undertaking it will sweep the world, and Lincoln's dream will come true. "A world without a slave or a drunkard in it." If we fail, it would set back one of the greatest moral tri-umphs of Christianity for a century. We are not going to fail. (7)

That same year, December 6, 1927, Dr. Wilson addressed the convention of the Anti-Saloon League of America at Washington, D.C, and the title of the address being "What Has Prohibition Done?" He began by admitting that Prohibition had not been 100 percent efficient:

> *Prohibition has not yet had a fair trial, for it ought to be in the hands of its ablest, strongest, and most aggressive advocates; and it has not been. It has not yet had a long enough time or a fair enough trial for any man to say it is a failure. It is entitled to as long a time and as fair a trial as the license system had, and I figure that that was about 140 years.*
>
> *Yet prohibition at its worst has proven itself to be better than the license system at its best. . . judge prohibition by what it was intended to do, and it has been a success.*
>
> *1. It has outlawed the liquor traffic in the United States of America; and*
>
> *2. Prohibition has annihilated the license system. The license system was worse than the saloon . . . [because it] was conducted by*

a Christian nation — that whole license system was wrong in logic and a failure in practice.

3. Prohibition has removed legalized and organized temptation from our streets. (A person) can get liquor if he hunts it, but the liquor traffic is not hunting him (or her) down. (Gladstone said) "It is the province of Government to make it easy for men to do right, and difficult for them to do wrong." Prohibition is fulfilling this function of good government.

4. Prohibition has made news of a perfectly normal thing in our American life. Drinking liquor and getting drunk was so common a few years ago that it had no news value. Prohibition has made news of a very common thing.

5. Prohibition has put the biggest liquor dealer the world ever saw completely out of business. Prohibition has converted Uncle Sam.

6. Prohibition has given us the greatest period of financial prosperity the world ever saw.

7. Prohibition has been the greatest clean-up in American politics of any single movement in the history of our country. The enthronement of the 18th Amendment and the Volstead Act (marked) a moral epoch in the upward trend of Christian civilization; and

8. Prohibition has totally transformed the

habits and the home life of America's liquor-drinking millions. If America stands true, makes good, enforces its law and demonstrates the dry policy to the other nations, we shall see not only in our day a dry United States, but a dry world. (8)

By 1929, public sentiment was turning against the "Noble Experiment," and Dr. Wilson himself came under increasing attack in the press. The closing four years of the Prohibition Era were difficult years for a man who had greeted the placing of the Prohibition law in the Constitution with such promise not only for the United States but for the world. One such critic of Dr. Wilson was the writer of an editorial in Plain Talk magazine in March 1929.

CHRIST AND DR. WILSON

Dr. Clarence True Wilson is supposed to teach the tenets of the gentle Christ. It is what he is paid to do. Does he earn his money? Recall what happened when Mary Magdalene came to Christ with her confession of sin. His luminous words of pity and forgiveness have come down the ages. Dr. Clarence True Wilson, impeccable body and impeccable mind, was not there to cast the first stone. But Dr. Clarence True Wilson has cast a cartload of bricks at the Michigan mother of ten children, who was sentenced to jail for life for possessing four pints of a liquid not greatly stronger than Jesus offered at Cana.

What does Dr. Wilson say? This, "Our only

regret is that the woman was not sentenced to life imprisonment before her ten children were born." And this, "When one has violated the Constitution four times, he or she is proved to be an habitual criminal and should be segregated from society to prevent the production of subnormal offspring." And this, "Prohibition is here to stay until the sun grows cold."

Apparently Prohibition is here to stay until the return of Christ. It has stayed until 1500 licensed saloons in Detroit have been increased into 20,000 speak-easies. It has stayed until a mother of ten children was thrown into prison for life. It has stayed until this preacher of Christianity has spoken some of the meanest words of a century. (9)

The alleged quotations of Dr. Wilson in Plain Talk magazine reflect a far harsher personality than that known by family and friends. Arthur Sears Henning raised the question, "Are the churches of America reaching out for temporal power?" Henning pointed to the steady expansion of the Federal Council of Churches of Christ in America into the area of political activity. Already a league of six Protestant denominations, representing thirteen million communicants, was attempting to make the will of the church, the will of the people. Henning claimed the power of the church to be greater than that of political bosses. "Churchmen make and unmake presidents, governors, judges, and national and state legislators. They shape domestic legislation and influence foreign policies."

Henning was greatly concerned about the growing power of the Federal Council, with its focus on issues of world peace, disarmament, national defense, immigration, labor, industry, and foreign relations. His other great concern was the political power of the national Conference of Organizations Supporting the Eighteenth Amendment. This organization was an amalgamation of thirty-three clerical and secular bodies, including the Anti-Saloon League and the Methodist Board of Temperance, Prohibition, and Public Morals.

He saw an interlocking within the Federal Council of pacifism and internationalism on the one hand, and on the other, the departments of prohibition in the six member denominations: Methodist Episcopal Church; Methodist Episcopal Church, South; Presbyterian Church USA; Northern Baptist Convention; Disciples of Christ; and Congregational Church. Henning accused the national dry conference of expending $250,000 annually in political activity. He claimed that Prohibition organizations had become a new invisible super government that governed by propaganda. He called it "the third house of Congress."

Henning claimed fewer than a score of clergy operated this church lobby. In the inner circle, it was the Methodist Episcopal Church that dominated. First among outstanding leaders of the church lobby was, according to Henning, Methodist Bishop Francis J. McConnell, president of the Federal Council of Churches. Of concern was McConnell's involvement with the National Council for Prevention of War and his role as president of the Methodist Federation for

Social Service, which Henning believed was leftist-leaning. Second on Henning's list was Bishop James Cannon, Jr., of the Methodist Episcopal Church, South, who was active with the Church Peace Union, as well as with the World League Against Alcoholism and the Anti-Saloon League.

Others on Henning's list were the Rev. Dr. Arthur James Barton of the Southern Baptist Convention; Bishop Thomas Nicholson of the Methodist Episcopal Church and president of the Anti-Saloon League; and Ernest H. Cherrington, Methodist layman and member of the executive committees of the Anti-Saloon League and the Federal Council of Churches. In addition, Henning named Bishop William F. McDowell, president of the Methodist Board of Temperance, Prohibition and Public Morals; and Dr. Clarence True Wilson, general secretary of the Board.

It was reported that Bishop McConnell was calling for the church through the proper organization of its influence to regain temporal power lost at the time of the Reformation. Past Federal Council president, the Rev. S. Parkes Cadman, depicted the Federal Council as the logical instrumentality through which the churches would achieve and exercise political power.

> The day is past when any realm of our economic, industrial, social, political, or international life will be regarded as outside the sphere of responsibility of the churches. All over the country prophetic voices are declaring from the pulpit and in ecclesiastical assemblies that the organized group life of society is to be no less subject to the rule of Christ than

the life of the individual. (10)

Henning went on to write of the influence of the dry lobby in election of Hoover to the Presidency. He reported:

> *As soon as Mr. Hoover was inaugurated they (the drys) held a meeting to map out their program for more and better Prohibition legislation and enforcement.*
>
> *As a result of its demonstrated power to make and unmake public officials, the Anti-Saloon League is the most feared agency of the church lobby... it was under the whip and spur of the church lobby . . . and the watchful eyes of Dr. Clarence True Wilson . . . that Congress . . . enacted the Jones Law making every violation of the national Prohibition law a felony punishable by maximum penalties of five years' imprisonment and $10,000 fine.*
>
> *One of the most efficient branches of the church lobby is the Methodist Board of Temperance, Prohibition, and Public Morals, housed in the Methodist Church building adjoining the grounds of the national Capitol. "This beautiful building," said the Rev. Dr. Clarence True Wilson, general secretary of the board, "makes Protestantism visible in the most influential capital in the world and answers every purpose in its constructions."*
>
> *The Methodist lobby is the envy of all other lobbies, with its representatives sitting on the floor of both houses of Congress. Six of the ten*

advisory members of the Methodist Board of Temperance are members of Congress: Senator Simeon D. Fess of Ohio and Representatives William C. Hawley of Oregon, Homer Hoch of Kansas, T. J. B. Robinson of Iowa, Addison T. Smith of Idaho, and John W. Summers of Washington. Occupying apartments in the Methodist building are Senators George W. Norris of Nebraska, Joe T. Robinson of Arkansas, and Carl Hayden of Arizona, and Representatives Philip D. Swing of California, John E. Rankin of Mississippi, and Homer Hoch of Kansas.

The board originated the form of propaganda represented by its famous clip sheet, a collection of observations on political and moral questions in which the church is interested, which is issued weekly for reproduction in newspapers as original editorials, and for use by preachers in their sermons. "One clipping agency," says the research secretary of the board, "has sent us in the past six months more than 4,000 clippings of our matter which has been reprinted or commented upon in the nation's daily press."It represents more than 40,000 inches of educational publicity. This is the report of one agency alone, covering only a portion of the daily press, but these clippings would fill an ordinary daily newspaper for forty-six days and the space at advertising rates would cost more than $100,000."

The Methodist board boasts of the possession of the most complete card index of Con-

gress extant. It contains "each congressman's name, his address, his religious affiliations, his fraternal affiliations, and his vote on every question of interest to us. Perhaps someone may ask why we have his religious and fraternal affiliations. Certainly not to use them to his detriment. We simply wish to have on record every fact which will aid us in understanding him and his probable action in any contingency."

These contingencies frequently arise, and the card index is invaluable in indicating to the Methodist lobby what religious and fraternal wires to pull when votes are needed in Congress. How the Methodist lobby operates in one of these contingencies is told in the March, 1927, issue of The Voice, published by the Board of Temperance. The bill to reorganize prohibition enforcement was threatened with defeat by filibuster in the closing days of the sixty-ninth Congress. The drys found themselves one vote short of the two-thirds necessary to apply cloture to the debate and thereby force a vote on the measure. The Methodist lobbyist consulted his card index. He espied therein the name of Senator Royal S. Copeland of New York, politically wet but recorded under "religious affiliation" as a Methodist. Thereupon the lobbyist appealed to Senator Copeland in the name of his church to give the vote necessary to victory. Senator Copeland complied, the cloture motion prevailed by a vote of 55 to 27, which was precisely a two-thirds majority, and the passage of the bill followed. (11)

The New York *Daily News* openly called Prohibition a "religion" in an editorial May 2, 1929, and labeled the Methodist Board of Temperance, Prohibition, and Public Morals a lobby.

> *Prohibition is a religion and it has become the state religion of this country. A part of the church discipline of the Methodists, Baptists, and certain other religious bodies, which the English call nonconformist sects, is that members shall not drink or dance or go to the theater and that they shall observe the Lord's day and keep it holy.*
>
> *The principle is a survival of time-honored austerities. It is a proper subject for any church body to concern itself with. Nobody can object reasonably to the practice of this principle by those who believe in it. Some of the best and strongest men and women in the United States subscribe to the doctrine and practice it in their daily lives.*
>
> *But there are religious bodies whose beliefs permit them to see nothing wrong in the moderate use of liquor. Wine, in fact, is an essential item in certain religious observances of the Jews. The Roman Catholic Church has never, so far as we know, forbidden its members to drink nor has the Protestant Episcopal Church. Yet the Methodist and Baptist churches have allowed most of their leaders to take this question from its proper sphere of re-*

ligion over into the sphere of politics, and to bully and blackmail an anti-liquor law into this country's constitution. That is an attempt to impose the religious beliefs of, say, two-thirds of this country's church people on the remaining one-third and the balance of the population. That is making Prohibition a state religion, in a country whose historic policy and basic law forbid any such thing.

There you have the reason why the Prohibition dispute breeds so much hatred. It is a religious question. And Prohibition cannot succeed, because you cannot put one-third of the population in jail, and there is no other way to cram a religious belief down those people's throats.

These remarks are given point by the fight between Senator Copeland of New York and Clarence True Wilson, boss of the Methodist board of Temperance, Prohibition, and Public Morals. Copeland showed considerable courage when he stood up and accused his own church of allowing its morals board to lobby at Washington. The interesting feature of Dr. Wilson's reply was that he admitted all of Copeland's charges; namely, that the board did "confer" with congressmen and senators on legislation in which the Methodist church was interested, and that it had sent a man to see Copeland about his vote in the senate on a cloture motion having to do with Prohibition.

Dr. Wilson went on to abuse Copeland for "playing politics" and being a poor Methodist.

> *This is a scarcely veiled threat of political reprisal. If Copeland is a poor Methodist, the word will be passed to the good ones to get out their tomahawks when he runs again. Dr. Wilson, by his own words, convicts himself and his board of morals of doing nothing under the sun but playing plain, everyday politics at the center of the American government. Such an activity has nothing to do with the Sermon on the Mount, the Ten Commandments, or the bread and wine. (12)*

Dr. Wilson wrote a lead article for *Collier's* in 1929, calling for a stronger enforcement of Prohibition law by the federal government. The article was titled "Send Out the Marines." *The Chicago Tribune* responded by asserting:

> The Reverend Doctor would not care for the marines . . . The American soldier is not low enough morally to raise the hell the reverend doctor would like to raise. (13)

Earlier in the month, the *Chicago Tribune* carried an article on "The Washington Gang and Its Work." At the convention of the American Medical Association in Portland, Oregon, the retiring president, Dr. William S. Thayer of Baltimore, deplored the centralizing tendency of government, saying it was breaking down local control and concentrating regulation and destruction of liberties in Washington. His special reference was to Prohibition, which even denied the physician's right to prescribe according to his judgment.

Dr. Wilson was vacationing in Portland at the time of the convention, and he took the opportunity of being on the scene of the convention to attack Dr. Thayer and the physicians who resented the Volstead laws. Dr. Wilson said that the Baltimore physician was a tool of the saloons and that the restrictions in the prescribing of liquor were necessary to keep bootleg doctors from carrying on a traffic in intoxicants.

The Tribune stated:

> "Dr. Wilson is one of the most active of the gang which controls Congress by bribery in the form of honoraria and by intimidation and otherwise has influence only with the ignorant and illiterate and because of them... a government is sought (by this gang) which will abandon the citizenship to the law of the church organized politically with its dictates as to what is orthodoxy and what is heresy. It will control opinion, destroy conscience and self-determination, and make men walk in moral chain gangs.... Dr. Clarence True Wil-son ... and the other political clerics whose demands are authoritative in Washington are the agents of this retrogression of democracy." (15)

Other newspapers and magazines joined in the name calling:

> "Is the Methodist Board a 'lobby' and is Dr. Wilson an 'arch-lobbyist?" asked *Time* magazine. (16)

In 1929, The Hearst Publishers sponsored the Hearst Temperance Contest. Most of those who entered supported the rapidly growing Repeal sentiment. Dr. Wilson entered the contest declaring that there is less drinking now than ever before. He stood opposed to government ownership of the liquor traffic. His plea was to give Prohibition a fair trial.

It is entitled to as fair a chance and as long a trial as the license system had and, when we have observed it and enforced it, if it does not succeed, it will be time to annihilate it. If it does succeed, all who believe in true temperance will be satisfied. (16)

As more news came of the activities of the bootleggers and the public was more and more calling for an end to Prohibition, Dr. Wilson called on the church to take a greater responsibility to educate for abstinence and to show respect for the law. "The church is responsible," he said "A still church is the bootlegger's hope." (17)

> After twenty years the task is not yet completed. We must reach a new generation. We must stress education. We must insist on law enforcement. We must keep pace with the latest research. (18)

The *North American Review*, in an August 1930 article by Ray T. Tucker, featured Dr. Wilson as the "Prophet of Prohibition."

> Dr. Clarence True Wilson is, without a doubt, the most sensational moral and politi-

> cal reformer of the United States. As the Senate Lobby Committee recently disclosed, the late lamented Dr. Wayne B. Wheeler, while legislative representative of the na-tional Anti-Saloon League, dominated Presidents, Cabinets, Congresses, and political conventions. Nevertheless, it was Dr. Wilson who set the stage for Brother Wheeler to do his stuff. Though Wheeler may have beaten the politicians at the Capital, it was Dr. Wilson who beat the tom-toms among the people. Since 1910, when he became executive secretary of the newly organized Methodist Board, he has been scourging the saloon in every State in the Union. While Carrie Nation fought with a hatchet, Dr. Wilson warred against rum with his tongue and tracts. (19)

Editorials in *The Christian Century* in December 1930 and March 1931 addressed the issue of the Methodist Board's presence in Washing-ton. The contention of the editorials was that the Methodist Board should get off Capitol Hill. In the view of *The Christian Century*, the Board of Temperance, Prohibition, and Public Morals had led the Methodist Episcopal Church suspiciously far into the field of political action. "Without doubt the Methodist Church has been and is now the most potent agency for moral progress, social reform, and better gov-ernment that exists in our American life." Yet in the view of the editors, it was the duty of Methodist opinion to adopt a more critical attitude toward an agency that presumes to speak in the name of the

Methodist Episcopal Church.

Does the Methodist Church, as such, desire to bring direct denominational pressure to bear upon the national government? There may be some types of churchmanship whose conception of democracy would not be affronted by such attempts at ecclesiastical domination of government. But Protestant Churchmanship would. Any such concentration of ecclesiastical officialism at the nation's capital goes against the instinct of American Protestantism.

> While a defense could be made for the presence of the Anti-Saloon League in Washington no such defense could be made for the Methodist Board of Temperance. This board as a political instrument is a fifth wheel in Washington. It renders no service by being there which is not better done by the Anti-Saloon League. On the contrary, it tends to confuse the situation and to divide the support which ought to be given to the one agency which represents the Prohibition convictions of all the churches... In the interest of our common Protestantism, we believe that the wedge which Methodism has unwittingly started to drive into American democracy should be withdrawn by the removal of the headquarters of its Board of Temperance, Prohibition, and Public Morals from the capital city. (20)

While others may have viewed the passage of the Eighteenth Amendment as a victory, Dr. Wilson saw it simply as a battle cry for action. During the thirteen years that the Prohibition Amendment and the Volstead Enforcement Act remained on the law books, Dr. Wilson worked tirelessly to educate for abstinence and respect for the law. Prohibition had popular appeal in light of the harmful effect upon families and society caused by problem drinking and alcoholism. However, government enforcement officers did not have much will for, or the funding for, enforcement, and while church folk were proud of the accomplishments of their Temperance Board, it was the least funded of any such organization.

The "noble experiment" was soon to end, and Dr. Wilson came under increasing attack by the press as popular sentiment turned against Prohibition. Regardless of how much the press disliked Dr. Wilson's stand on Prohibition and his political activism regarding enforcement, they were unable to cast any doubt upon his character.

This in contrast to Bishop James Cannon, Jr., who headed the work for the Methodist Episcopal Church, South. Cannon was attacked in the press and investigated by his own church for playing the stock market, unethical business ventures, and an alleged extra-marital affair. (21)

With Dr. Wilson, what you saw and heard was what you got. He was a devoted family man, he loved his church and his country, and he believed with all his being that Prohibition, given a chance, was the best possible answer to the liquor problem—for America and the world.

Now for a close look at Wilson's unlikely friendship with the agnostic Clarence Darrow.

Wilson called Darrow the best friend he had known since the death of his father.

— 8 —

Darrow and Wilson: Best Friends

One of the most remarkable friendships was that of Dr. Wilson and Clarence Darrow. This was about as unlikely a match as could be imagined. Darrow and Dr. Wilson were to travel the United States and Canada from coast to coast debating the issue of Prohibition versus the license system. Before Dr. Wilson met Darrow in person, he went to the Darrow home in Chicago. Mrs. Darrow greeted Dr. Wilson at the door. Clarence Darrow was not at home. After Dr. Wilson explained who he was and expressed his interest in a meeting with Darrow, he received the following response from Mrs. Darrow: "I can not possibly see what you and my husband would have in common."

The March 27, 1930, the Northwest Edition of *The Christian Advocate* carried an editorial on the Wilson-Darrow debates entitled: "The Two Clarences Find a Way."

> Said a reader the other day, "What did you mean when in last week's paper you seemed to call for a different sort of dry strategy?" And while he asked, Clarence True Wilson and Clarence Darrow were supplying the answer.

They were appearing in several Eastern cities, holding debates on Prohibition.

The spectacle of the two Clarences in bloodless duel offers opportunities which such a sports writer as Westbrook Pegler could by no means overlook. That aspect of the incident we leave to his wholly competent pen.

But these debates illustrate admirably a part of what is involved in our appeal for more imaginative and popular dry campaigning. Why can't we give human nature a chance, even in a fight?

This is exactly what makes the Darrow-Wilson debates so refreshing. They operate to transform the dry attack from a Spanish Inquisition to a crusade. Instead of either partisan resorting to rack, thumb-screw, and boiling oil, the Christian Richard can have at the infidel Saladin and in turn be rushed, each combatant cherishing a wholesome respect for the other.

They meet on equal terms. They are bound to believe in one another's sanity, sincerity, and patrio-tism. The wet must give the dry full faith and credit; and the dry must be similarly disposed toward the wet. Several happy results are sure to come from such encounters as these.

For one thing, each debater has a better chance to reach people of opposite opinion than he could get by occupying the platform alone. Dr. Wilson has con-firmed more Methodist conferences in their dry faith than any other man. But even he can make few converts at an annual conference. The unregenerate wets do not frequent such gatherings.

And confirmed drys do not flock to hear Mr. Darrow when he is a solo performer. Why should they? But the debate draws both sides. In part they come with the hope of seeing their favorite score an-other triumph against the hated foe. But quite as much they come for the sheer human love of watching a struggle of Titans. So do thousands go to a football game who have never seen the campus life of either university?

Another welcome value of these debates is their recognition that Prohibition is still a debatable ques-tion. Many wets have reached the point where they refuse to think of drys except as snoopers, grafters, sadists, and hypocrites. Many drys talk as though an opponent of the Volstead Act were of necessity a guzzler, a lawbreaker, and in general a shameless child of the devil.

These plainly prejudiced attitudes cannot be held if you agree to debate on one side or the other. Nor can they be blindly cherished if you consent to listen while the debaters argue. You concede that each side has a case, though, of course, you may still believe that the side you favor has much the better case.

One other highly important profit which the de-bate method produces is that it directs the attention of both sides to methods which do not involve the use of force. It is high time that the folly of more and yet more force were seen by wets and drys alike.

This country is not going to abandon Prohibition merely because the law is broken with increasingly daring contempt. That sort of force cannot drive the American people from a course which it believes right. If Clarence Darrow has arguments by which he can convince his fellow citizens, well and good. He has far better chances of succeeding than have a thousand Al Capones, no matter how strong they may be with timid or corrupt politicians.

And this truth applies to the dry side also if and when enforcement measures seem to the observant citizen to be developing into a combination of fear and tyranny, that day the dry cause will be facing defeat. It is far better that Clarence Darrow, with all his famous powers as an advocate, should be standing up to a dry champion than that he should be defending in court a gang of killers who have done to death their rivals in an outlawed trade.

It is far better that Clarence Wilson, with all his practiced genius at showing Prohibition as a thing to live and die for, should be employing his powers before an audience half indifferent or even hostile, than that he should be urging congressmen to contrive Prohibition laws increasingly drastic and difficult of execution.

Everybody knows that President Hoover

> was right in calling Prohibition an experiment. And so it will continue to be, until the conscience and judgment of the American people are more stabilized on the subject than they are now. The Wilson-Darrow debates aim at that stabilization, rather than at the terrorism which never can prevail in this country, whether its source is gangland or the Federal Capitol. (1)

A debate in Baltimore, May 13, 1930, was the first in a series to be held on successive nights in Wilmington, Philadelphia, Trenton, Newark, and New York City. The *Baltimore Post* pictured these two wordy foemen as the best of friends.

Clarence Darrow intimated to the Rev. Clarence True Wilson today that he plans to discard verbal kid gloves in their debate tonight on the question, "Resolved: That Prohibition Is Right in Principle and a Success in Practice."

The noted lawyer, who has abandoned his practice to champion the cause of civil and moral liberty, met the executive secretary of the Methodist Episcopal Board of Temperance, Prohibition, and Public Morals at the Altamont Hotel for the "weighing in" ceremonies preparatory to their public debate at the Alcazar ....

Though Dr. Wilson and Mr. Darrow are warm friends personally, they have yet been unable to agree on any subject more controversial than the weather, and their brief periods together invariably end in a verbal tangle on moral issues.

Dr. Wilson had run over from Washington to welcome Mr. Darrow and make him comfortable, and while this was in progress Mr. Darrow, in response to a reporter's question, opened up on his friendly enemy:

"The Volstead Act is to blame for all the killings, all the bad liquor, and all the menace to human liberties today.

It is purely the work of fanatics who have neither a sense of justice nor mercy.

They would gladly prescribe the death penalty for taking a drink.

They will keep on infringing on freedom as long as the people will stand for it.

They will not stop until they have Prohibition of card-playing, Sunday amusements, dancing, theaters, and even smoking ..."

"Prohibition is the work of fanatics," Darrow said. "Most of them have no justice, sense, or mercy. They would gladly give the death penalty for taking a drink."

It was a swift uppercut, but Dr. Wilson sparred. "We're not quite as bad as that," he said. "But we believe the violation of the prohibition law is as serious as the violation of the burglary law."

"Yes," Darrow answered, "there you have it. You consider drinking a crime. Pretty soon these same fanatics will make some new crimes out of dancing, card playing, and Sunday movies."

"Not at all," Dr. Wilson answered. "The whole trouble is Prohibition has been enforced

so loosely no one knows its possibilities. Recently a policeman lost his job and will be tried for manslaughter because he fired on a bootlegger who put up a smoke screen when he was trying to get away.

"The policeman would have been commended if he had fired on any other criminal. Of course, I do not believe in killing, but I think there should be a better balance of justice."

And Darrow's answer was, "Dr. Wilson, you would make a good lawyer." (2)

A news report on the Wilson-Darrow debate appeared in the *Evening Journal*, Wilmington, Delaware, May 14, 1930, as follows:

WILSON AND DARROW DEBATE PROHIBITION

"I'm for the saloon and any other place where I can get a drink."

Clarence Darrow, internationally known criminal attorney and Prohibition abolitionist who will take part in a debate in the Shubert Playhouse tonight, was speaking.

His bald statement in favor of the saloon was made in reply to Dr. Clarence True Wilson, general secretary of the Board of Temperance, Prohibition, and Public Morals of the Methodist Episcopal Church, who will debate with Mr. Darrow in the Shubert Playhouse tonight.

Dr. Wilson and Mr. Darrow were seated

this afternoon in the office of Robert W. Priest, manager of the Shubert Playhouse. Around them stood several friends, including Josiah Marvel, David Snellenburg, and State Senator W. A. Simonton.

While speaking generally of the subjects to be discussed at tonight's debate Dr. Wilson said that in all his experience with anti-Prohibitionists he never met a "wet" who favored the return of the old-fashioned open saloon.

"Well, here's one who is," interrupted Mr. Darrow. "I'm in favor of the saloon and any other place where I can get a drink."

Dr. Wilson said the question to be debated tonight is: "Resolved, that Prohibition is right in purpose and successful in practice." He will take the affirmative and Mr. Darrow the negative.

Mr. Darrow referred to the Jones Act, signed by President Coolidge just before he retired from the presidency as the "five and ten cent act."

The act provides for sentence up to five years and a fine up to $10,000 for persons convicted of selling, manufacturing, or transporting liquor, all of which offenses are felonies under the act.

He said the Prohibition law is "the acme of bigotry and intolerance."

Concerning President Hoover's appeal for observance of the Prohibition law, Mr. Darrow had this to say:

"Mr. Hoover is an engineer and not a

philosopher."

Mr. Darrow doesn't believe in Prohibition, he doesn't believe in the church, he doesn't believe in immortality, capital punishment, and he has vast disbelief in just about everything Dr. Wilson does believe in.

Dr. Wilson is undoubtedly the most spectacular oratorical defender of Prohibition and is just as prominent in his way as Darrow is in an entirely different way. He has a reputation of being a convincing speaker, and one who wins the sympathies of his audience, while Mr. Darrow is incisive in his style and known as one of the best criminal lawyers in the nation. Those who hear the Darrow-Wilson debate will probably come away with just about as thorough an under-standing of both sides of the question as one could get in a single evening. (3)

These East Coast debates made news across the country. On May 14, 1930, the following article appeared in the *Oregon Journal*, in Portland, Oregon.

DARROW, WILSON DEBATE DRY LAW

Baltimore, Md., May 14—(Universal Service)—Brickbats and bouquets were tossed at Prohibition Tuesday night when Clarence Darrow, noted lawyer, and Dr. Clarence True Wilson, secretary of the board of temperance, Prohibition, and public morals of the Methodist Episcopal Church, locked horns in debate here.

Arguing the question, "Resolved, that Prohibition is right in principle and a success in practice." Darrow also launched a vicious attack against the Methodist Church, terming the headquarters of Dr. Wilson's organization, opposite the Capitol in Washington, the "Methodist Vatican."

Dr. Wilson, in the beginning, refused to claim Prohibition had dried up all sources of supply of liquor and contended lawlessness was not the result of Prohibition because the liquor traffic always has been lawless. He cited the following benefits:

The liquor traffic has been outlawed in the United States.

The saloon has been annihilated.

The American license system, "that picked up souls of citizens for revenue," is gone.

Legalized temptation has been taken away from men.

Prosperity has resulted after a great war for the first time in the history of the world.

Dr. Wilson's statement that "There was not a drunk in the house or senate," was greeted with derisive laughter. It increased when he said, "the old soaks are gone."

Darrow opened his argument by saying a Prohibitionist had a great advantage over a wet—he can make up his facts as he goes along. No matter how foolish they are, other Prohibitionists will believe him.

He attacked each of Dr. Wilson's state-

ments, especially the one regarding post-war prosperity, saying: "I wouldn't trade my individuality for all the gold you could pile up. When men talk of exchanging freedom for dollars, they are either bigots or crazy."

The prosperity resulted, he declared, from high wages during the period immediately before and after the United States entered the war—when men had what they wanted to drink.

Darrow then attacked Dr. Wilson's organization, demanding to know what its activities "as a board of public morals had been during the oil scandal." Members, he declared, were "hypocrites—plain, square, dishonest hypocrites." Dr. Wilson's office was termed the "Methodist Vatican, across the street from the capitol, where weak-kneed congressmen and senators can be bulldozed and awed."

Darrow then declared more girls and women were drinking than ever before. Saying he had drunk "a little" for 45 or 50 years, he added:

"I would rather a man go to hell free than to heaven bound. I never will permit anyone to pass a law in my case telling me what I can drink. When people can be bulldozed into giving up liberty for fear of jails and fines, then we are going back on the road to slavery."

In rebuttal, Dr. Wilson declared only now had Prohibition a chance to show its worth.

"The wrong kind of men were appointed to enforcement positions under the Harding ad-

ministration," he said. "Coolidge was straight, clean, non-committal, and non-acting. He made no mistakes and no moves. Now proper enforcement is at hand."

Prohibition, he concluded, was entitled to the 150 years of experiment that had been accorded the license system. (4)

A rather entertaining report of the Wilson-Darrow debate in Detroit vas reported as follows in the *Detroit Evening Times*, May 28,1930:

DARROW, DR. WILSON CLASH ON PROHIBITION

Holy writ, the "Methodist Vatican," the Pennsylvania primaries, the back room of the old-time saloon, stealing, and Clarence Darrow's declaration that "Prohibitionists may be willing to wait for their fun until they get to Kingdom Come, but I'm not."...

All these things entered into a debate last night in Orchestra Hall between Darrow, who says the first reason he is against Prohibition is that he likes to drink now and then, and Dr. Clarence True Wilson, the nation's leading terror of evil-doers, whose official title is executive secretary of the Methodist Board of Temperance, Prohibition, and Public Morals.

Darrow and Doctor Wilson have been traveling together for some months, somewhat in the Chautauqua fashion, debating Prohibition up and down the land.

Darrow says that if Dr. Wilson was not a Prohibitionist he wouldn't be a bad sort. Dr. Wilson says if Darrow wasn't so frightfully obstinate on the subject of Prohibition, he might make a good Methodist.

Last night Darrow sat on the right hand of Robert D. Wardell, executive secretary of the Michigan Modification League, and Dr. Wilson sat at the right hand of the Rev. R. N. Holsaple, superintendent of the Michigan Anti-Saloon League.

Judge Alfred J. Murphy of Circuit Court was the master of ceremonies. The audience was large and well behaved except for two brief interludes when Doctor Wilson was booed and even hissed. Once was when Doctor Wilson said Prohibition had cleaned up politics, and the other time was when he said Prohibition had caused ten years of unparalleled prosperity.

Both of the stars made speeches; neither indulged in debate as Webster defines the word. Prohibitionists and anti-Prohibitionists in the audience did their best to outdo each other in the volume of hand-clapping, giving the affair somewhat of the complexion of an amateur night when the boy or girl who gets the most applause wins the celluloid kewpie.

The "debate" was sponsored by the Pisgah Lodge, No. 34, Independent Order B'nai B'rith.

Here were some of Darrow's remarks:

"Just think of the name of Doctor Wilson's

organization and weep. In the first place what has Prohibition to do with temperance? He calls his bunch the board of 'Prohibition, Temperance, and so forth.' You can't have Prohibition and temperance.

"And then he adds, 'Public Morals/ Are Prohibitionists concerned with public morals? Lord, No! They don't object if a man steals, robs the government, or swindles his country. All they want to know is whether a man is wet or dry and if he's dry, they put a halo on his head. They don't give a continental about either temperance or public morals.

"These Prohibitionists get their pleasure out of life by taking all the pleasure out of mine. They want to force me not to drink. I wouldn't try to force them to drink. It would be a waste of good liquor, because it would take too much to make them human.

"Did you ever hear of a really intelligent man who didn't drink?

"If Christ lived today Prohibitionists would send him to Atlanta for turning water into wine, and if they learned about the wine at the last supper they'd put poison in it.

"Doctor Wilson defends the idea that the government should poison liquor. He gleefully quotes Doctor Doran's statement that after all no one was ever poisoned who didn't violate the law by drinking whiskey. My God, are we going to poison men for drinking? I tell you Prohibitionists are the most cruel, barbarous, and sadistic men who have lived since the in-

quisition.

"Doctor Wilson says we have the best and purest Congress in history. I say we never had so many cheapskates making the laws of our country. There used to be a man named Webster in the Senate and he knew more drunk than all the drys know sober. Henry Clay was some fellow and he took a drink. Andrew Jackson was a man of parts and he sometimes drank too much. There were a lot more of them.

"Prohibitionists have one track noses. They can smell a drink but they can't smell oil. The Methodist Vatican is so close to the Capitol it couldn't be closer. Did they ever bat an eye at the oil scandals? Did they ever show concern for public morals in that hideous piece of lobbery? No. They were asking public men the bigger question—'Do You Drink?'"

Doctor Wilson's remarks included the following:

"It is true that we support men who drink wet and vote dry. But many a man stands for higher things than he lives up to. He may drink himself but he knows drink is not for the public good.

"The people are irrevocably committed to Prohibition. Why, in Pennsylvania they have nominated Gifford Pinchot, a dry of the drys, for governor.

"It is as silly to say Prohibition is a failure as it would be to say the laws against stealing should be repealed because some men still steal. It is the purpose of law to make it easy to

do right and hard to do wrong.

"Taking saloons from the streets and driving the liquor out of politics is the greatest achievement of mankind.

"The liquor traffic, like a chicken with its head cut off, is dead but doesn't know it yet.

"If there is as much drinking as there used to be, why aren't there so many drunks in the street?

"There is not one old soak left in the United States Senate. The last one left eight years ago.

"In this day of motors, the drunken driver is a menace. The old days when a drunk could be loaded in his buggy and his mule could be depended on to find the way home, are gone.

"Women and children are no longer exposed to the saloon environment. Uncle Sam is taking a joy ride on the water wagon. (5)

October 11, 1930, the Wilsons and Darrows were together in Great Falls, Montana, where they inspected the art work of Charles M. Russell. Dr. Wilson was first to inspect the works of Russell and other Western artists on display at the Mint. After spending nearly half an hour in the Mint during which time Mr. Willis traced for him the history of Russell and explained many of the paintings of Western life, Dr. Wilson expressed the desire to have the rest of his party see the exhibit.

"I am very much interested in the history of Montana and have read two books on vigilante days," said Dr. Wilson. "These pictures and curios here in the Mint aid me to visualize those days."

The entire party returned with Dr. Wilson later in the day at the Mint. Asked his opinion of Russell's art, Darrow inquired whether it was not possible that the great artist might have taken a drink now and then. Informed that there was such a possibility, Darrow said: "He must have. Anyone able to portray on canvas such scenes as we have inspected must have had to live the life of the West. Russell knew the West and he certainly had the ability to preserve it on canvas." (6)

The Great Falls debate took place in the high school auditorium Saturday evening at 8 p.m., sponsored by the Lion's Club. A large crowd was reported to have heard the debate on the Prohibition question. The major parts of their talks were obviously meant to entertain the audience.

Dr. Wilson stated in his opening remarks that Prohibition had achieved the most marvelous results of any legal enactment in the last 140 years. He said it wiped out the old liquor license system in which men "paid money for the right to do wrong." It removed temptation from the young and those without will. He declared Prohibition helped avert depression, because money which would otherwise have been spent after work for liquor was diverted into other channels. Prohibition has caused the last ten years of prosperity, he said.

Dr. Wilson contended the dry law had cleaned up politics and related his first visit to Congress, when the sergeant-at-arms showed him eighteen members of the Senate who were drunkards. Now 94 percent of the members of both Houses of Congress are church members, he asserted. Caucuses in saloons have been stopped.

Darrow opened his speech with the declaration that "The drys never did care much for brains," and that Wayne B. Wheeler, heading the Anti-Saloon League, and the Methodist Board of Temperance were always able to smell alcohol around the Capitol, but little else. They let the oil scandals of the Harding administration slide by without a murmur, Darrow said.

"Drinking is an old and respectable habit," Darrow declared. "Most great men have been drinking men. Did you ever see a poem written on ice water? That is what they used for writing sermons. Christ would be in a Federal prison if he lived today, for his miracle of changing water to wine."

The leading lights of what Darrow called "The Methodist Vatican in Washington" could "see no causes or effects but that they are all caused by liquor and this world fills their whole horizon of thought." (7)

Following the Great Falls debate on October 11th, the men were on the move with other debates throughout the West: October 13th in Spokane, Washington; October 15th in Seattle; and October 17th in Dr. Wilson's home city, Portland, Oregon, where he was warmly received by family and friends. The press, however, was more favorable to Darrow. Following the Portland visit, the next day they debated in Boise, Idaho, and on October 19th in Salt Lake City. a day later, they debated in Denver, and on October 21st, they were in Omaha.

From Omaha they moved to Milwaukee, Wisconsin, October 24th; Cincinnati, October 27th; and Indianapolis, October 28th. En route to Milwaukee, Dr. Wilson managed to give two speeches in Mankato, Minnesota, at the state Sunday School Convention. [Most likely the author's father, who lived a few miles away, heard Dr. Wilson speak on this occasion.]

The first week in November, the Wilson-Darrow debates moved to Galveston, Houston, and San Antonio, Texas. From Texas the team returned to the East Coast with a stop en route in Anderson, Indiana. This remarkably speedy trip was all by train with both men's wives also along. (8)

An interesting report of a Wilson-Darrow debate appeared in a Seattle newspaper.

> Whichever side the auditor was on, he went away satisfied his cause had carried off the honors. "What does Wilson know about saloons?" said Darrow. "He was always lounging around churches... Prohibitionists have a one-track mind, if any. It is just as bad to eat too much as to drink too much. Prohibitionists are against having fun."
>
> Wilson claimed Prohibition has brought us honest politics. When the crowd began to laugh he continued, "It may not be so in Seattle yet! But it's headed your way."
>
> "I stand for liberty, and when the flag of my land ceases to stand for liberty, I am for liberty and not the flag," said Darrow. He continued, "The old spirit of Puritanical intolerance never dies. Prohibitionists want not only to shoot people who sell us a drink, they want

to poison us who drink it." (9)

The Seattle Star gave the debate to Dr. Wilson. The paper reported, "Respect and admiration of the Methodist leader grew as the debate progressed. As a scalper, he got one last night." Dr. Wilson declared the Ontario liquor dispensing system a step backward. Darrow hailed it as a long stride toward liberty and tolerance. (10)

In Boise, Dr. Wilson told reporters of his friendship with Darrow. "Oh! I enjoy him immensely. He is the most colorful, most delightful, most kindly, most loving, and adorable man the nation has had since Roosevelt and Bryan. It is really worth the punishment he deals out to me in the debates to get to accompany him on our tour." (11)

In Salt Lake City, Dr. Wilson was viewed by the press as "a leading figure in the fight against strong drink." The Wilson-Darrow debate was held at the Hotel Utah. At the speakers' table were Senator and Mrs. Reed Smoot.

Dr. Wilson said, "Liquor interests have caused disregard for the law from the time of the 'Whiskey Rebellion' in 1794 and throughout the period of licensed liquor selling. When statistics are brought in, the biggest liar wins. The benefit of Prohibition has been that the liquor traffic has been outlawed."

To this Darrow replied, "Prohibition has not removed the temptation. I can still find liquor-selling places. Everyone knows it but the doctor here. Both drinking and gluttony have killed people. The Prohibition Drys do not pass on candidates with their minds, but with their noses. If the candidate's breath smells of liquor, they turn him down." (12)

In Omaha, Dr. Wilson declared, "There will be no modification of the Volstead Law." He was, however, alarmed at the inactivity of the drys. "Get rid of Prohibition and you'll get rid of the gangsters," was the view set forward by Darrow. (13)

A Kansas City newspaper viewed "The Two Clarences" as "a most successful vaudeville team." Darrow attacked Dr. Wilson and "the Methodist Vatican at Washington as the most brutal, bigoted, ignorant bunch since the Spanish Inquisition," while Dr. Wilson said, "Prohibition is the miracle of the twentieth century. It has overthrown a vicious traffic that dominated the nation, has made the liquor dealer a cringing bootlegger. Prohibition is here to stay. We may live to see the world dry. Every nation on earth is looking to us with hope."

To this Darrow replied, "Wilson has the advantage over me. He makes his history as he goes." Darrow continued, 'Ten men go down to gluttonous graves to every man who goes down to a drunkard's. I prefer the drunkard's grave and I would have a better time getting into it." (14)

Dr. Wilson and Darrow debated October 23, 1930, at the Ivanhoe Temple in Kansas City. From there they moved on to Milwaukee. The debate there was viewed by the Milwaukee Sentinel as a wet victory by eight votes to four. "We got rich (after the war) out of the wreck of the world, and Dr. Wilson says it was because we didn't drink," said Darrow. "Personal rights should not take precedence over the public welfare," said Dr. Wilson. Darrow invited Dr. Wilson to see some speakeasies. "If you want to see the speakeasies, change your clothes and I will show them to you." (15)

The press in Galveston, Texas, portrayed Dr. Wilson as "a champion of teetotalism; in other words, a bone dry, to whom the word liquor is anathema. To the drys Prohibition is a sacred issue, closely akin to religion." (16) *The Galveston Daily* quoted Darrow's famous one-liner: "Prohibition has made a madhouse of the United States." (17) In Houston, Dr. Wilson told reporters: "I have come to greatly admire Darrow. I have a kind of affection for him like I used to have for my father. Darrow is always for the underdog. He is not religious but he has all the qualities a religious man seeks to cultivate." (18)

When a crowd of 6,000 came out to hear Darrow debate Dr. Wilson in Houston, Darrow looked out over the crowd from backstage and said to someone, "Do you know why such a large crowd? They came to see an infidel." During the debate Darrow said, "I don't ask a Prohibitionist to take a drink with me; it would be a waste of perfectly good liquor. With a Prohibitionist it's a religious question. It's sinful to take a drink. You are supposed to go to hell for it."

Darrow, speaking of the Methodist Board in Washington, said, "The Methodist Vatican in Washington is between the depot and the Capitol so they can smell Congressmen's breath on the way to the Capitol."

Dr. Wilson told reporters, "I am going to meet Mr. Darrow on the platform only because I know I am right and he is wrong." (19)

By mid-November, the Wilson-Darrow tour had moved on to Washington, D.C. A human interest article in the "In This Neighborhood" column in the *Daily News* reported Darrow's visit to the Methodist Building.

> *Clarence Darrow yesterday went on a tour of inspection of the Methodist Building, the white stone structure adjacent to the Capitol grounds, which he has so often referred to as the "Methodist Vatican." The famous agnostic's guide and escort was Dr. Clarence True Wilson, chairman of the Methodist Board of Temperance, Prohibition, and Public Morals, often designated by Darrow as the Methodist Pope."*
>
> *Darrow was here to take part in the four-cornered religious debate at Washington Auditorium with Rabbi Abram Simon, Jew; Quin O'Brien, Catholic; and Rev. Jason Noble Pierce, Protestant.*
>
> *Sound movie cameramen arranged a scene between Darrow and Dr. Wilson, as the former entered the building. "So this is the Vatican," said Darrow. "I am glad to meet you at your home. It appears to be quite a stronghold."*
>
> *"I am glad you think the Vatican is dry enough to compare it with this," said Wilson.*
>
> *"See you took pains to locate it close to the seats of the mighty," observed Darrow. "It is too bad that this road separates the Vatican and the Capitol. Don't you have to dodge drunken drivers when you walk across the street near your quarters?"*
>
> *"Not since prohibition," remarked Wilson.*

"I suppose you heard about the election," said Darrow.

"Yes," said Dr. Wilson, "it seems there was an upset. But the drys still have three-fourths of both the House and Senate."

"You fellows are mighty optimistic," said Darrow.

"It looks like we have more right to be optimistic than the Republicans have," replied Wilson.

"Yes," was Darrow's retort, "the Republicans wouldn't have any optimism if they didn't have you." (20)

A news story from Houston on November 19, 1930, called the two Clarences "Strange Friends: One who has devoted his life to spreading the gospel of God and of temperance ... the other who questions all religion and vigorously assails Prohibition."

"I love that man, he is the greatest humanitarian in all this country ... He has the biggest heart and kindest feelings of any man I have ever known," said Dr. Wilson of Darrow. (21)

The support for Prohibition came mostly from small town and rural America. When Dr. Wilson and Darrow debated in Boise, October 18, 1930, the *Capital News* gave the vote to Dr. Wilson over Darrow.

The Darrow-Wilson Prohibition debate Friday evening in the high school auditorium under the auspices of the Bonneville Club, was not only interesting and entertaining but just a little disappointing, too— disappointing because Clarence Darrow, the celebrated criminal lawyer of Chicago, not only did not measure up to the expectations as an orator in the minds of many in the audience, but he was clearly out-pointed in the debate by his opponent, Dr. Clarence True Wilson.

Dr. Wilson anchored his argument to a century long fight against the manufacture and sale of intoxicating liquors bringing the controversy up to date to the passing of the eighteenth amendment and the agitation that is now underway to repeal it. The essence of his argument was that Uncle Sam for many years dominated and humiliated by the liquor traffic, had finally asserted his manhood and placed a perpetual ban on that traffic. He did not use statistics but his argument was forceful.

Mr. Darrow confined himself largely to ridicule and satire and witticism. He based his plea for repeal of the eighteenth amendment on the grounds strictly of personal liberty and the right of the average citizen to go about his way and exercise his individual right without interference. He scorned church interference with personal rights and directed his attacks against the Methodist Episcopal church.

Both speakers were courteously received by a large audience and liberally applauded. If anything, that applause was more in favor of Dr. Wilson's argument than Darrow's. Dr. Wilson opened the debate for thirty minutes, followed by Mr. Darrow for thirty minutes, after which Mr. Wilson was allowed twenty minutes for rebuttal and Mr. Darrow thirty minutes. The last ten minutes was given to Dr. Wilson for closing.

In appearance, the two debaters were strikingly different. Dr. Wilson, white haired, neatly dressed, suave, a forceful but clear speaking orator, stood out in contrast to Mr. Darrow, slightly round shouldered, with black, grayish streaked hair hanging somewhat in disorder over his forehead, sharp featured, with little attention given to dress. (22)

Here is the way the debate looked to the *Capital News* critics:

FOR DARROW
By Therman R. Evans

"I'm against Prohibition," declared Clarence Darrow, one of the ablest criminal lawyers in the nation, in his opening speech of the Wilson-Darrow debate Friday night. "When I want a drink, I don't want anybody bothering me. Prohibitionists don't want to drink and they don't want anybody else to drink. I don't care enough about liquor to want to make a Prohibitionist drink. It would be a waste of liquor. It would waste a lot of good liquor to try to make a good fellow out of a Prohibitionist.

"The only thing I'm interested in not having is the present system of bootlegging," Darrow stated emphatically. "There are too many tra-

ditions of freedom in this country to tolerate interference with personal liberty. Sooner or later, Prohibition will work out its own destruction.

"What's the matter with liquor?" Darrow suddenly asked the audience. "It has an old and distinguished lineage, dating back to the earliest age of man. Man makes the grape juice. All nature needs is a chance.

"If we take away everything that has ever been written by men who drank, all that would be left of the world's vast store of literature would be Baxter's 'Saints Rest' and Bryan's 'Prince of Peace.'" Good liquor is a part of the world's literature, art, science, philosophy. Imagine trying to write a poem on a pitcher of ice water. A Prohibitionist couldn't write a poem or paint a picture, not even a fence or a barn—he wouldn't have imagination enough.

"Leave man alone. Let him be free to fight his own battles. He will do well; he will do ill. In the end he'll die anyway.

"If you take liquor from the world, all the genius and intelligence and imagination will be crushed out by your murderous touch.

"My learned friend fails to remember that the juice of the grape is a part of the creed of every faith—except the Mohammedan. Why, the first miracle ever performed by Jesus Christ was the turning of water into wine at the wedding feast in Cana. If I were a Christian, I would be afraid I'd go to hell for repudiating the action of the founder of my own

religion. If Jesus Christ came to Boise and did what he did in Cana, my learned friend and Senator Jones and others would send him to federal prison for five years.

"Let him live and let me live," Darrow pleaded in his closing remarks. "There is no reason to poison my cup and to forbid me to drink. That's pure tyranny. Why can't wet and dry live in a spirit of tolerance, kindliness, and good will to their fellow man? It's hard to make people agree on anything, so why try?

"You work your side of the street and I'll work mine and we'll both be happy." (23)

FOR WILSON
By Laurene Thomas Smith

Dr. Clarence True Wilson, debating that "Prohibition is right in principle and a success in practice, and should be maintained," cleared the minds of many on this great issue and easily, proudly won. The decision was against Clarence Darrow who had the negative side of the argument. And in winning Dr. Wilson impressed those of his audience who might have read Bruce Barton's What Can a Man Believe? as the ideal minister of a hundred years hence.

Dr. Wilson has personality plus. He is a handsome man, a cultured man, a forceful man, and a most convincing man. He is just the sort of man people instinctively know is far, far above the average in every way. That he should debate against the leading criminal lawyer of the world is just too bad for the criminal lawyer, regardless of his rank, for Dr. Wilson in taking the side of Prohibition had an ideal to fight for, whereas the lawyer has but a defense to make of an outworn custom.

Dr. Wilson's dramatic plea at the close of the debate, "Give Prohibition at least as long a trial as license liquor has had before you condemn it," summed up a long argument in favor of Prohibition. He started out, being the first speaker, by saying that he believed Prohibition is right in principle and a success in practice. He admitted that it is not one hundred percent efficient, nor perfectly enforced, nor universally observed, but that, he said, is no reason why it should be repealed. Just because there is a traffic accident is no reason for erasing a yellow line which marks the spot where cars are to stop or go, he said.

"As long ago as 1794 liquor has been a problem of this country," he said. In that year the "whiskey rebellion" was put down and "free rum" was the issue of the bitter fight. So, he pointed out, the present crime situation did not start with Prohibition.

"Prohibition is the greatest moral triumph of the 20th century," said Dr. Wilson, "for it has outlawed liquor traffic in the United States. Liquor, which in the past ruled us, controlled politics, city councils, everything, even to the election of presidents, can do none of these things now for it is outlawed and on the defen-

sive. Legalized temptation has been removed and now it is easy for men to do right and hard for them to do wrong.

"The purpose of our constitution was to promote the general welfare. This means to give the citizens life, liberty, and the pursuit of happiness. We discovered after a while that the pursuit of drinking happiness that brought misery to families was unfair, unjust, and unrighteous and this government by revoking the liquor license is extending life, liberty, and happiness to the women and children of the land. Our fathers ordained and established the constitution of the United States to secure the blessings of liberty to ourselves and our prosperity. The more license the less liberty. The blessings of liberty have always come to free men regulated by law to which they yield a loyal obedience," he said.

"No inherent right of the state has been transgressed by Prohibition. It is the state legislatures themselves that have amended our federal law. The states lose no police power; they have the same right to prohibit liquor traffic they had before, but they cannot go into partnership with a trade which is naturally and inherently immoral and illegal.

"Prohibition at its worst is better than the license system ever was or ever can be at its best," he said emphatically. "A man can violate the Prohibition law or any other law, if he chooses. But stealing does not prove that there should be no law against it."

Dr. Wilson's side of the debate was not without its humor but his jokes were more subtle than those of his opponent. For instance he referred to a "relative" of his who had formerly been in the liquor business. The "relative" was "Uncle Sam," who was "up to his neck in the liquor business, making millions of blood money —but now Uncle Sam is taking a joy-ride on the water wagon."

He admitted that one thing the drys have over-looked was putting over an educational campaign after Prohibition was on the statute books. That responsibility is just as much an obligation for the wets as the drys, he says, for we are all bound to vote for public welfare. 'The liquor traffic is an altogether different problem than the 'private appetite.'" He referred to the "freedom and individual liberty" of Robinson Crusoe, who had absolute personal freedom before Friday appeared upon the scene—and after that his "personal liberty" was somewhat curtailed.

He quoted the Japanese adage, "A man takes a drink and the drink takes a drink and the drink takes the man."

He scouted the suggestion that Prohibition is not the will of the American people and challenged anyone to find a better way to get the majority vote of the people than the method used for the eighteenth amendment. Out of 96 legislative bodies in the 48 states 93 of them ratified the amendment and only 72 were actually needed to put it over. He urged a "saloon-

less land" in which to raise American children. He pictured clearly the benefits accruing from Prohibition and challenged his opponent to deny them but they were unanswered. Wets and drys alike admire Dr. Wilson tremendously for his stand in the debate. He was most convincing and the Methodists and all church people can be proud that such a man heads the temperance movement. (24)

In 1932 Darrow and Dr. Wilson were in Richmond, Virginia, once again debating the Prohibition question. Darrow called the drys a bunch of morons. Dr. Wilson said Prohibition had been good for the country. Darrow said, "Prohibition has given the country the greatest set of crooks and incompetents the government has ever known." Dr. Wilson said, "Jesus did not make wine but grape juice." He got a laugh on that. He said, "We have a tacit understanding in these debates that Mr. Darrow shall amuse and I shall give the facts." Darrow said, "Dr. Wilson, you would make a good lawyer," and Dr. Wilson said to Darrow, "If soundly converted you would make a great preacher!" Dr. Wilson was credited with never losing his temper in a debate and achieved a reputation as a pulpit and platform orator. (25)

It may have been a mistake in strategy for Dr. Wilson to debate Prohibition with Darrow. Sentiment was turning away from Prohibition, and while Dr. Wilson remained convinced that Prohibition was best for the country and, having been enthroned in the Constitution, was here to stay forever, his willingness to debate the issue with Darrow did give recognition that Prohibition was still a debatable question. Yet, in the long run the debates and more especially the deep and abiding friendship between the two men perhaps mellowed Dr. Wilson and, in turn, the nation to accept the fact that alcohol was here to stay. The most that could be hoped for was a strictly regulated industry, along with a moral appeal for abstinence, or at least moderation, which is what the term "temperance" originally meant. Certainly Dr. Wilson learned, as others have, that there are those who drink alcohol, as Darrow did, without bringing untold misery to self and others. The fact that Dr. Wilson called Darrow the best friend he had known since the death of his father shows that his hatred for the harmful effects of uncontrolled drinking did not stop him from counting a moderate drinker among his friends and, more than that, a person for whom he had the highest admiration. The witness of this friendship was of far greater significance than the content of the debates. It was to be the beginning of the long process of healing following America's "second civil war," the first over slavery, the second over so-called "demon rum."

While the two Clarence's had differing views of liquor control, they were to develop a close friendship during their travels in Ontario.

— 9 —

Study of Ontario Liquor System

During the year 1930, *Collier's* sent Darrow and Dr. Wilson to Canada to study the Ontario Liquor System. When they issued their joint report to Collier's, published September 27, 1930, they were in agreement upon one point—"that it is hopeless for wets and drys to agree." Even when presented with the same facts, the Prohibitionists and the anti-Prohibitionists were poles apart in their conceptions of government, individual rights, and the purpose and perplexities of life. Each saw the problems of society and the nature of mankind from an entirely differing viewpoint.

They did agree that the Dominion of Canada is made up of nine provinces and that the province of Ontario, chosen for their study, was in many ways similar to the United States. Ontario established the system of governmental control of liquor after the election of 1926. The Ontario laws permitted only government stores to sell liquor as a beverage. Each year the sale of liquor had regularly increased. Liquor was sold at a very reasonable price. Each year the government issued annual permits to Ontario residents and monthly permits to tourists.

The study team found the universal opinion among all classes of people that the liquor control was honestly administered by the Control Board with a view of promoting temperance. They found bootlegging on any extensive scale to have been wiped out in Ontario. What little bootlegging remained consisted in the selling of small amounts after closing time or to persons whose permits had been denied. (1)

It was reported that Dr. Wilson and Darrow had a delightful time together on their travels in Ontario. Darrow did not seem to "wear horns and smell of brimstone" and Dr. Wilson turned out to be an "affable, good-humored, and open-minded gentleman."

The prohibition law of Ontario went into effect in 1927. Prior to that time the Dominion had passed an act which permitted the provinces to provide for local option. Strict liquor legislation was in place during World War I. Even with government control following the 1926 election, three-fourths of the geographic area of Ontario remained dry through local option laws. After June 1, 1927, only government stores were permitted to sell liquor as a beverage. All buyers of liquor were required to have a permit book. Such permits could be canceled by the Liquor Control Board at any time.

Liquor was to be consumed only in the buyer's home, not in transit, or in any public places. All advertising of liquors was forbidden. The 120 government stores in the province of Ontario were open from 10 a.m. to 6 p.m. on week days, closing at 1 p.m. on Saturdays, and for the entire day on Sundays, holidays, and election days. (2)

Dr. Wilson again made the cover of the October 4, 1930, *Collier's* with his article, "And the Drinking Was According to the Law." Dr. Wilson began by stating his view that Canada was making an honest effort to solve the liquor problem. The claims of the extremists proved untrue. Dr. Wilson and Darrow did not find drunks staggering in the streets.

The Canadian system was designed to promote home drinking instead of public drinking. A man must carry his drink to wherever he claimed to call home. And there he could drink to his heart's content. Dr. Wilson looked upon almost all drinking as a male activity and was alarmed that men would be drinking in their homes in the sight of women and children. In the Canadian home "the drinking" now "was according to the law."

A second design of the liquor control system was to get rid of the liquor influence in politics. What Dr. Wilson saw in the Ontario system was not liquor influence out of politics but a complete partnership of liquor traffic and the government. In his view it was not "government control, but rather a government controlled by liquor interests."

Bootlegging was still to be found in Canada. Government regulations, if designed to discourage drinking, had not done so. Gross sales in government stores were on a steady increase. Dr. Wilson speculated that if the per capita consumption of liquor continued to increase, Canada might well soon be drinking more than any other nation in the world's history.

What Dr. Wilson saw during his 1930 tour of Ontario was a church that was walking softly on the liquor question, and temperance organizations there were making little noise. But these groups, Dr. Wilson believed, were not blind, nor did they lack courage. They were biding their time. Everything was going the way of the liquor interests, but he believed conscience that was then slumbering would soon be awakened by the sight of universal drinking. He wrote:

> The fact that the temperance organizations are not demanding immediate repeal of government control does not mean that they are satisfied with the situation. On the contrary, they believe that the inherent weak-nesses of the system will eventually destroy it, that time is its greatest enemy. (3)

In the November 1930 issue of *Twentieth Century Progress*, Dr. Wilson summarized his views on the license system in Canada. He reported:

> The system is a success—
>
> 1. If the desire is to furnish cheap liquor to the consumer...
> 2. If the object is to furnish relatively safe liquor... there are comparatively few cases of poisoning except by ethyl alcohol. Upon the other hand, alcoholism has increased.
> 3. If the desire is to control distribution by the establishment of a paternalistic system which discriminates between individuals and dictates in personal matters.

4. If the purpose is to suppress evidences of public drinking and prohibit trade promotion by advertising and display ...
5. If the plan is to discourage public discussion of the liquor question.
6. If it is the intent to suppress "big" bootlegging ... The government itself has taken their place...
7. It is hoped to promote the financial interests of the brewers, distillers, wine makers ...
8. If the object is to increase the output of intoxicants—the intake per capita, to make buying and selling and drinking respectable, patriotic, and well nigh universal, then the system is doing all that they could wish.

But the system is a failure—

1. If the intention was to eliminate private profit.
2. If the intention is to divorce the liquor trade from politics...
3. If the intention is to decrease the liquor bill...
4. If it is intended to discourage the consumption of whiskey...
5. If it is the intention to suppress drunkenness...
6. If it is intended to suppress other offenses usually associated with consumption of liquor...

> 7. If the purpose is to decrease accidents in the handling of machinery ...
> 8. If the object is to decrease the number of breaches of the liquor law ...
> 9. If the object was to keep drink out of the homes .... (4)

Dr. Wilson backed each statement with facts and figures. He believed that Canada would soon return to prohibition and that the two neighbor nations of Canada and the United States would stand in friendly handclasp looking forward to a better age of peace, prosperity, and sobriety, "according to the law." (5)

Clarence Darrow had a different view of the Ontario Liquor System, which he filed with *Collier's* under the title "Let No Man Therefore Judge You in Meat or in Drink." While Dr. Wilson told readers why he thought it bound to fail, Darrow gave his reasons for considering it a great achievement.

He reported:

> Quietly, decently, Ontario drinks, respecting its government and a sanely administered, enforceable law. Across its border, a nation of lawbreakers get its liquor by crime, bribery, and contempt of government. (6)

Darrow was convinced that at least 80 percent of the voters of Ontario believed their government control method of handling the sale of intoxicating liquors was much better than any other that had been tried in Canada. Darrow saw no drunkenness in Ontario. He reported:

> Ontario has less signs of drinking than any other section of the world that I have ever seen. (7)

Still, Darrow admitted, there was much about the law that did not appeal to him. He did not like the idea of having to buy a bottle of liquor at a government store and then go straight home without sharing his treasure with a friend. It almost seemed he had to go right home, hide in his room, and drink the whole bottle right away.

While the two Clarences had differing views on liquor control, they were to develop a close friendship during their travels in Ontario. All of Dr. Wilson's prejudices against Darrow melted away in the presence of such a kindly, gentle man. Darrow enjoyed a joke on Dr. Wilson as they were traveling from Ottawa to Toronto. As they drove through a quiet town, Dr. Wilson remarked that there didn't seem to be much business going on. Darrow was quick to remind Dr. Wilson of what he had strangely forgotten, that the day was Sunday. Darrow suggested that he might sing some hymns to refresh Dr. Wilson's memory.

Dr. Wilson noted in writing about Darrow his abstemiousness in eating. Darrow, it seemed, despised the gormandizer fully as much as Dr. Wilson despised the drunkard or the drunkard-maker. One thing Darrow could never forgive in William Jennings Bryan was his rather excessive eating, while Darrow himself, making no profession of temperance, was through life very abstemious both in eating and drinking. (8)

The report of the Ontario system in Collier's by two opponents, yet friends, offered an alternative for American citizens to consider. Dr. Wilson's objections to the Ontario control system were carefully thought out and documented. Many of his objections could well be applied to post-Prohibition liquor control methods in the United States. Darrow, on the other hand, made little use of statistics but depended on his charm and what seemed to many a common sense approach regarding human nature. That the two men had such great respect for each other shows that in their heart of hearts they must have seen some bit of truth in each other's views.

March 23rd, 1933
Dr. Clarence True Wilson
I want to tell you that it would take much more than a difference of political or social questions not to continue to respect and love you.
Your friend always,
Clarence Darrow

— 10 —

Repeal: Bitter Aftertaste (1933-1936)

On April 7,1933, President Roosevelt signed the so-called Beer Bill that allowed for the sale of 4 percent beer while the prohibition of hard liquors still remained in force. Dr. Wilson wrote regarding the signing of the Beer Bill:

> Thomas Jefferson signed the Declaration of Independence, Washington the Constitution and the Farewell address to the American people. Andrew Jackson signed the anti-nullification paper to South Carolina, Abraham Lincoln signed the Emancipation Proclamation, Woodrow Wilson signed the Armistice; Calvin Coolidge signed the Kellogg Peace Pact, and Franklin D. Roosevelt signed the Beer Bill. (1)

Dr. Wilson was greatly disappointed when Roosevelt signed the Beer Bill, yet he denied saying anything bad about Roosevelt. He still believed that if the people would only confirm their support for continued prohibition of all alcoholic beverages that President Roosevelt would enforce the law of the people.

Sadly for Dr. Wilson, however, the public turned away from Prohibition as one state after another ratified the Twenty-First Amendment. Michigan had been the first to ratify the amendment for Repeal on April 3,1933. The required number of states ratified the amendment by December and the Repeal Amendment became law, replacing the Eighteenth Amendment and ending the "Noble Experiment" at 3 p.m., December 5, 1933.

The Washington Post pictured "Prohibition's Friends and Foes as New Liquor Era Dawns." Flanking a picture of President Franklin D. Roosevelt were the personages who stood out prominently in the battle against national Prohibition. They were Rufus S. Lusk, Mrs. Charles H. Sabin, Alfred E. Smith, James A. Farley, William H. Stayton, Albert C. Ritchie, and Janett Shouse. Those pictured as prominent figures in the fight against Repeal were Dr. Wilson, F. Scott McBride, Ella A. Boole, Bishop James Cannon, Jr., and Senator Morris Sheppard. (2)

Earlier in the year when it was already apparent that the Repeal movement was winning, Dr. Wilson received a most sympathetic letter from his dear friend and debate opponent, Clarence Darrow.

Clarence Darrow
1537 East 60th Street
Chicago

March 23, 1933
Dr. Clarence True Wilson—

I have thought of you a good deal in the past weeks. Don't think that I shall gloat over the wet victory. I have fought in so many lost causes, that I know how the other fellow feels. You have always been sincere and honest in your work and have done the best you could. I don't believe that any political question can be handled to the satisfaction of anyone who has such fixed ideas as you and I have long had. We are just obliged to make the best of the situation. Perhaps it will not make any great difference to most people. What we need is work to keep our minds away from the petty troubles of life. Of course I have always believed in temperance, and have practiced it very well. At least until you think there is another chance to accomplish what you want, I hope you will keep on educating the people to real temperance; that is, practicing it in eating and drinking. Anyway, don't take it too seriously; one can't get much out of life unless he can make the most out of what he has. I want to tell you that it would take much more than a difference of political or social questions not to continue to respect and love you. Perhaps we might find a chance to run in that Harpers Ferry trip. There is a matter on which we are sure to agree. Sometime I shall be in Washington again and will go and see you. With our best wishes to Mrs. Wilson and yourself—

Your friend always,
Clarence Darrow (3)

What a tribute of true friendship. More than fifty years after her father's death, Maribeth Wilson

Collins read a hand-written copy of this letter to the author of this biography. The re-reading of that letter brought tears to her eyes. It was obvious that the friendship between these two men, and their families, had been of a quality seldom seen among mortal beings.

Dr. Wilson proclaimed Repeal as the worst blow to the country in one hundred years. It was also a strong blow to Dr. Wilson. He was to suffer from failing health much of the remaining few years of his life. Family members reported observing that Repeal simply took the wind out of his sails and he never really fully recovered. Nevertheless, he did not leave the battlefield.

Sunday evening, January 3, 1934, Dr. Wilson was at Lincoln Avenue Methodist Episcopal Church in Pasadena speaking on the subject, "Where the Twenty-First Amendment Leaves Us" and "What the Drys Plan Next."

> *The 21st Amendment leaves the 18th in Repeal and the liquor traffic will start on another career. Its rights imbedded in the Constitution of the republic, it is singled out for special mention as preeminent above all other enterprises. It will come back full powered. The distillers will reopen their works, the brewers will start business and inaugurate the reign of the brewers' association. The saloon, the gambling den, and the brothel will all be in evidence and the brewers will make common cause with any of the three that get into trouble with the decent element of the community.*

We shall have saloons and brewery-owned saloons. We shall have bartenders and the town drunks again. We shall have an equal proportion of women and men drinking, and barmaids as an additional attraction. We shall have the liquor traffic in politics, defeating every decent man who runs for office. It will invade business, competing with every honest business man and lessening his profits by the full measure of the liquor traffic's receipts. We shall see the poverty and drunkenness, the neglected homes and little children condemned to live and grow up in a saloon environment which starts them toward criminality before they are conscious of it.

Every law which we once had for the regulation of the traffic has been shot and the laws that we afterward enact will be violated by the most lawless of all mankind—the keepers of the saloons and the accompanying evils. This organized traffic will put its brand on judges, sheriffs, district attorneys, and give us the kind of politics that used to reek like sin.

So the public is going to open the flood gates of booze in the Machine Age, with airplanes over our head and automobiles and traffic jams in our streets. Nothing like liquor can make a good auto driver a menace to society. Every auto in the world will be just as drunk as its driver. An automobile with a drinking driver is a deadly weapon. The nut that holds the steering wheel must keep sober.

The blind populace stampeded by the wet

press and the crooked politicians is rushing madly on to unregulated liquor selling. But they are due for a rude awakening by a visitor through our roof at night with the whole place smelling of liquor or our little girl crushed on the sidewalk by a drunken driver. This will bring our people to their senses just a little too late. And the fool farmer who is too busy to vote against Repeal will have his milk orders cut fifty percent, for the beer bottle always crowds out the milk bottle.

The 21st Amendment goes into the Constitution and will ruin a dozen great industries that the selfish may have their beer at the expense of home and trade. "Man shall not live by beer alone." With the 18th Amendment gone, the conscientious anti-liquor men will start a new program of more basic, personal, and social education against alcohol, which is a habit-forming, irritant, depressant, narcotic drug, detrimental to the human system in its every function, not even satisfying the appetite for drink. An inebriate was asked, "Haven't you had enough yet?" "No, often had too much but never had enough," was his reply.

We must shift our emphasis from law enforcement to personal conduct and create a conscience and an intelligence against drinking. We must teach the public that the manufacture, sale, and purveying to the public of intoxicating liquor in a tense machine age is not a business but crime and that crime ought not to be embedded in the Constitution of this republic. With multiplied thousands of airplanes over our heads and twenty-six million automobiles on our streets and highways, we should have steady nerves and clear brains, and will have them or get the consequences of our folly. All temperance organizations will have to revamp their programs; in some instances change their very names and reach out for the leadership of edu-cated young vigorous minds and start a no-drinking crusade. Perhaps the words "total abstinence" and "prohibition" will be largely eliminated but "no drinking" as a safe rule and the utmost possible restriction upon the engulfing liquor traffic will be the motto of the reform.

The schools must be made to obey the law of the states in teaching the effects of alcohol, narcotics, and opiates upon the human system. We must create a public conscience and a sentiment in harmony with the best interests of the human race and make public welfare predominate over dollars, especially the Al-mighty dollar that we do not have.

This unbridled craze for getting rid of Prohibition and inaugurating a reign of rum will bring its experience of bitter regret. It will be disappointing to the money-made people who want dollars circulating again. It will not look well in history that the administration of high-grade men should have openly threat-ened the states that did not help to repeal with the withdrawal of patronage.

The liquor traffic has never been a financial

help to a community, state, or nation. It will not balance the budget or pay our taxes. The reestablishment of it will be disappointing as a tax measure, foolish as a financial investment, and a Judas Iscariot deal in morals. "It is the province of government to make it easy for a man to do right and difficult for him to do wrong." It is therefore the height of social folly to organize temptation for men, women, and children and collect revenue out of debauching them. Many a parent who has referred to Prohibition as a joke will pay the balance of their lives by furnishing a drunken son or what is worse, a drunken son-in-law as the inevitable consequence of reopening the licensed liquor store. Many a farmer too busy to vote will find the beer bottle has come back at the expense of the milk bottle and the billion dollar fruit and vegetable business suffers the competition with beer and every other industry will be under the handicap of competing with that trinity of evils, the red-light district, the gambling hall, and the saloon, all of which may be expected back with beer. The church must get back to its work of moral suasion to save the drinker and his family. The depen-dence of its members upon law and the loss of spiritual concern for the man accounts for its failure to hold the conscience of the country. "The letter killeth but the spirit giveth life." What this country needs is the N.R. A. —a NATIONAL RELIGIOUS AWAKENING. The loss of the 18th Amendment and the failure to observe and enforce it was a symptom of a moral slump on the part of the people and a religious decadence. This generation will not live to see it again. There will be a dreadful reaction against the reign of rum but it can be blocked by thirteen states and we will not get national Prohibition while the generation is on earth that lost it. We should never attempt it until we have secured at least forty states and demonstrated that we can influence and make the people want to observe the law. We must go the long road back. No drinking, voting the saloon out of our communities away from our schools and churches, local option by towns, by the county unit, Prohibition by states, but let the problem be worked out by states until forty of them have made good. (4)

Following Repeal Dr. Wilson still held popular appeal with many who saw Repeal as a mistake and longed for the return of Prohibition. On December 9,1934, Dr. Wilson was speaking at State Street Methodist Episcopal Church, Camden, New Jersey. Introduced as a "long recognized front-rank leader of the Dry cause," Dr. Wilson told the assembly that the liquor problem must be solved properly. "It is a moral problem. We must go the long road back. We must make a moral appeal to save the drinker and his family. We must recreate an individual conscience against drinking and drunkenness." (5)

Dr. Wilson viewed the loss of the Eighteenth Amendment and the failure to observe and enforce it as a symptom of a moral slump on the part of the people and a religious decadence. (6) He was quick to pick up on Roosevelt s term for the new politics of economics of his administration, which Roosevelt named the "New Deal." Dr. Wilson used this term for the new work in temperance reform. As early as November 17, 1933, speaking in the evening service at St. John Methodist Episcopal Church, Seaford, Delaware, where he had once served as pastor, Dr. Wilson outlined a "new deal" in the work of temperance reform. "The church must change its emphasis from political, commercial, and legalistic arguments back to moral appeal." (7)

Dr. Wilson wasted no time in beginning a "new deal" in temperance reform. He told audiences that perhaps the words "total abstinence" and "prohibition" will be largely eliminated by "no drinking" as a safe rule and restriction upon the liquor traffic will be the motto of the reform. (8)

Legalized liquor again is on the way out, declared Dr. Clarence True Wilson when he spoke at churches in Youngstown, Ohio, March 3, 1935. He predicted that sentiment was growing against the reign of rum and he believed history would repeat itself. "The doom of the liquor trade will come quicker than it came before," he said. Dr. Wilson continued, "Repeal has not solved the liquor problem." He blamed President Hoover as much as President Roosevelt for the failure of Prohibition. In Dr. Wilson's view, "The groundwork for Repeal was laid in the Hoover administration. Repeal has hit business a solar-plexus blow." The liquor problem remained, in Dr. Wilson's view, "The Unrepealed Problem." He saw saloons making money that movies, real estate, grocery and dry goods merchants used to get. "It was a shallow brain that said that the first step to get the country out of the depression is to license liquor," he said.(9)

Everywhere he talked he told listeners to start from the bottom, teaching a new generation that "alcohol is a habit-forming drug." Traveling with Dr. Wilson on his post-Prohibition tours was Colonel Frank B. Ebbert, one of the three men who wrote the Volstead Act. Ebbert was viewed as the person who would rewrite the act. He outlined a three-step program:

> 1. The total elimination of the profit motive for liquor sales;
> 2. Suppress all publicity that would stimulate liquor business; and
> 3. Regulate and control the first two steps by amendment.

Ebbert told audiences, "Ninety percent of the evils today can be removed by these steps." (10)

Speaking in Canton, Ohio, March 6, 1935, Dr. Wilson made his strongest statement regarding the end of Prohibition.

> Prohibition will not come back. It is over and done with. We must move forward by educating the people along temperance lines. The beverage poison traffic is organized temptation. The license system is no remedy for the depression. It is lame in logic and a failure in practice; wrong in principle, and powerless as a remedy; fool's bargain in finance and a Judas Iscariot in morals. The license system

> is a crime against mothers and children. The liquor industry is a blood sucking leech among industries; it is a legalized outlaw; to license it is to coin buzzard dollars to lay on closed eyes of a nation's dead conscience. (11)

In Dayton, Ohio, April 2, 1935, Dr. Wilson said, "Reputable society could have prevented Repeal but it turned yellow in the moral crisis and did not vote." He continued, "Much of the agitation for Prohibition will rise from drunkenness at the wheel of the automobile which makes a car 'a deadly weapon'... but when Prohibition returns it will find another generation that will make of it a different kind of Prohibition." (12) "Liquor is the poor man's burden and the rich man's relief from extra taxation," he said. (13)

Sunday, May 23, 1935, Dr. Wilson was in Portland, Oregon, speaking at First Methodist Episcopal Church in the morning service and at the Central Methodist Episcopal Church in the evening. On Monday morning he spoke before the Portland Methodist preachers of the district regarding "The Unrepealed Problem."

> There will be a dreadful reaction against the reign of rum. Sentiment is changing. We cannot continue piling up drunken driving accidents, deaths, nor can we sit quietly by and see our children being made the victims of a trade that is determined to capture their appetites for the sake of untold profits. Perhaps a new strategy is called for, but the problem remains the same—alcohol. (14)

During the winter and spring of 1935, Dr. Wilson and Colonel Ebbert had launched a new drive to regain Prohibition. They conducted fifty-nine meetings in only thirty-four days of travel in Ohio and from there visited cities in New York. The temperance crusader team supported the Cooper Bill that would prohibit radio and newspaper advertisements of liquor. Dr. Wilson declared, "Prohibition was not tried under Harding and Hoover; it was just betrayed." (15)

During a tour of Wyoming and Montana in June 1935, Dr. Wilson said:

> I would have little to say if repeal solved the problem. But repeal has not solved the problem. The moral people must take an interest in this problem, and the specialty of the Church is morals. The Church, therefore, must major in this problem. If Prohibition was wrong it will stay in the grave; if it is eternally right it will have a resurrection. (16)

Speaking in Butte, Montana, June 19, 1935, Dr. Wilson said, "Repeal was the worst blow to the country in one hundred years. Where 150,000 drinking places were in the United States before Prohibition, we now have 500,000 since repeal." (17)

More optimistic at St. Paul's Methodist Episcopal Church in Helena, Montana, Dr. Wilson declared, "I expect to live to see our country completely and permanently Dry." (18)

Dr. Wilson addressed his last Methodist General Conference session at Columbus, Ohio, in May 1936.

Also speaking on the liquor issue were Roy L. Smith, Harold Paul Sloan, and George Mechlenburg, who declared Prohibition would be back in ten years. May 4 was set aside as Temperance Day at the General Conference. Dr. Wilson spoke to the conference assailing the theory that moderate drinking is harmless.

> I never knew a man to stop liquor, to break the habit, or even get over drunkenness by the moderation route. I do not believe it ever has been or ever can be done. Total abstinence is the only cure. (19)

Scientific research, along with the future experience of millions who would win over addiction through Alcoholics Anonymous, would prove Dr. Wilson right. Abstinence is the only known cure for alcoholism. What Dr. Wilson failed to understand was that not all users of alcohol were to be viewed as being in the same category with the alcoholic or problem drinker. Dr. Wilson's friend Clarence Darrow held to the view that moderate drinking was harmless. For him, and others like him, this may well have been true.

In Dr. Wilson's view Roosevelt broke faith with the American people in signing the Beer Bill. While Dr. Wilson could see that national Prohibition would not come back for a generation, he still saw the wet-dry issue playing an important part in the 1936 election. He pointed to the fact that automobile deaths were on the increase. He saw an urgent need for education in the schools regarding "the evils of drink." (20)

As Dr. Wilson continued speaking engagements during this post-Prohibition era, he began to review the mistakes that had been made. The federal Prohibition law had been passed with only thirty states behind it. That was a mistake. There should have been forty states behind the cause for national Prohibition. Dr. Wilson began talking of a movement toward a new kind of Prohibition. But at times he seemed reconciled to the fact that the battle was forever lost. One reporter quoted Dr. Wilson as saying in 1934, "Never again, in my opinion, will there be national Prohibition in America." (21)

Speaking in Blackwell, Oklahoma, Dr. Wilson said that temperance reform had been given a stunning blow but was not dead! He said, "We will not ask for Prohibition again until forty states are ready to back it." In his address he listed four doors that must be opened. In the row of doors he saw the church school, the public school, the Methodist conference course of study for ministerial ordination, and scientific textbooks on the effects of alcohol. Temperance reform education must take place behind each of these four doors. As to the seriousness of the problem he said, "Alcohol addicts outnumber other addicts by one hundred to one!" (22)

Dr. Wilson gained not only national but international acclaim for his work in temperance reform. In 1933, *The Town and Country Review*, published in London, carried an article about Dr. Wilson:

> A penalty of fame, attained in any sphere of public life, seems to be the manner in which humorous anecdotes, often entirely apoc-

ryphal, are tagged onto the famous. The Rev. Clarence True Wilson, one of America's foremost preachers and propagandists in the cause of temperance, is no exception to this rule, and the stories told of him are legion. One, which may be founded on fact, since he is interested in dairy farming, is that one day he had occasion to empty his pockets of temperance tracts when close to the stall of a prize Guernsey cow, noted for her enormous production of milk. The animal sniffed at the leaflets, nibbled a few of them, and the next day went dry as the State of Kansas during Prohibition. Whatever truth there may be in the foregoing, it is certain that Dr. Wilson's work for temperance in America has been remarkably effective; there can hardly be another man in the States who has held so many street meetings, park meetings, factory staffs, etc. enthralled, or addressed so many crowds from a touring automobile ...

Since 1912, under the direction of Dr. Wilson, the Board of Temperance has circulated fifty million leaflets, its secretaries have traveled 300,000 miles, total abstinence work has been established among Negroes, a publication has been established which goes every month to 28,000 Methodist preachers, a news service has been organized, over twenty notable surveys and sociological studies have been added to the literature of temperance reform, text-books and other books for class study and popular reading to the number of

> over 74,000 have been circulated, and it is estimated that Dr. Wilson has personally addressed a million and half people during the past four years. Dr. Wilson has been National Secretary of the Board of Temperance, Methodist Episcopal Church, since September 1, 1910. In addition to being widely known as a platform lecturer of great power and oratorical abilities, the Rev. C. T. Wilson is the author of many books on temperance. (23)

Beginning in 1916 and continuing to 1936, from the vantage point of the Board of Temperance, Prohibition, and Public Morals with offices in Washington, D.C., Dr. Wilson fought the battle with one goal in mind, that being to outlaw liquor from the face of the nation, if not the entire globe. He worked to advance this goal through four stages:

1. When the liquor traffic was in control;
2. When temperance forces grew strong enough to pass the Eighteenth Amendment;
3. During Prohibition he worked for enforcement and respect for the law; and
4. After Repeal he continued to warn of the consequences. (24)

The battle had not been an easy one. The record shows he continued to travel and speak and lead the country on the long journey back. Yet, he had his doubts. At times he hoped to see Prohibition return in his lifetime; at other times he admitted it would not return for a generation —or for one hundred years—and sometimes he would say, "Prohibition will never return."

Dr. Wilson did have his hobbies and other interests, but most of his life's energy had been devoted to temperance reform and Prohibition. It was only through the support of his admirers, the friendship and encouragement of his opponent Clarence Darrow, and the grace of God that he was able to make his way through those difficult days. The disappointment, the pain, and the pent-up emotion of the defeat of the "noble experiment" was to linger on for a generation or more in the life of the Methodist Church and other church bodies and temperance organizations that had devoted their all to the temperance cause. Only recently have the wounds begun to heal and energy return for new answers to the alcohol problem and the increasing drug problems of a new generation.

A world of love and friendship and tolerance, instead of bigotry and narrowness, would be worth living in. I'd like to try it for a thousand years.

— 11 —

Wilson the Writer

Professionally, Dr. Wilson was a writer as well as an orator. In addition to countless articles, essays, and reports, Dr. Wilson managed to write books. Perhaps the masterpiece of all of Clarence True Wilson's books was his biography of Bishop Matthew Simpson, published in 1929, in the Methodist Publishing House's "Makers of Methodism" series.

The title was *Matthew Simpson: Patriot, Preacher, Prophet.* Simpson was born June 21, 1811, in Cody, Ohio, was elected bishop in 1852, preached President Lincoln's funeral sermon in 1865, and blessed the nation's Centennial Exposition in Philadelphia in 1876. He died June 18, 1884. "On both sides of his family Matthew Simpson not only inherited good blood but also a wealth of good Christian Principles." So wrote Dr. Wilson. (1) Simpson studied medicine, considered law, and then felt a calling to ministry. His mother was overjoyed at a decision for ministry. "What a blessing is a sainted mother! I do not know what would have become of me if I had not had a praying father and mother," said Simpson. (2)

His career as a circuit-riding preacher did not last long. New realms were opened before him as president and founder of Asbury University in 1839 and editor of the *Western Christian Advocate* in 1848. "Simpson, the leader, patriot, and reformer, could not resist the opportunity of becoming editor of a great Christian paper." (3) "Wherever Simpson was placed, the same self-sacrificing and Christian character marked his career." (4)

He was a young man, only forty years old, when he was elected bishop. When he attended the General Conference in 1882, it was with thirty-two years of service as bishop, the oldest both in life and in years of service. "No other Bishop of the church ever had greater administrative power than he had. It was Simpson's firm belief that culture and education were essential to the advance of the church." (5)

"For thirty-two years he crossed and recrossed the continent, going into the lowliest little chapel, into the most magnificent edifices, and passing beyond the seas, that his voice might influence men to God in more distant lands and everywhere with the same result: thousands were thrilled with his mighty words and powerful delivery. It is doubtful if any man has exercised a greater power for good than he did, this leader of Methodism." (6) More than any other, with the exception of his father, Simpson was Dr. Wilson's model of a minister.

A popular tract published by Dr. Wilson in 1931 spoke of his concern regarding the growing trend of liberalism in the Methodist Episcopal Church. "What Ought the Conservative Do?" was its theme:

Methodism has very little of the divisive

spirit which attends extreme Fundamentalists, etc. Glad to be first a Christian who builds on the whole gospel and second a Methodist... just a Christian on the trail that has been blazed by John Wesley. Seen much of our doctrinal significance pared down to suit an unbelieving world. Ritual does not ring as true. The Conference course lacks the positive note present when it was selected by our Bishops.

What to do? We have not been given responsibility for writing the ritual or the course of study. If he is a conservative, he never will have the chance. A few things we can do without harm.

1. Our enemies have undercut the authority of the Bible. We can be a daily, nightly, student of it till it masters us, so that your soul is saturated with the immortal message and your preaching drips with it. When we are filled with the message of our Savior they will cling to us like iron filings do to a magnet.

2. Paring down of our great doctrines. Let the men who have a gospel still preach it with such power that souls will be converted under their ministry. If man with a half-gospel can get as many souls converted etc., we have nothing superior to that. To know by fruitage has the Savior's sanction. "Show me the quality of thy faith by the effects of thy work, and I will know who to follow and what to believe."

We need a revival. The soul must be

brought from its love of the world and of the flesh and of self and of sin to love Jesus Christ and to worship Him with clear minds and a heart of complete adoration and a life of supreme surrender to His will. We need a revival that will turn our churches from a dress parade of baptized worldlings to an army of fighting, marching, determined captors of this, our World Citadel in the name of the Father and of the Son and of His Spirit. We cannot get this revival by talking about it, but we can have it by going after it. I am going to join the band that wins the souls, that stands against worldliness, sensuality, and devilishness in every community life. If the Modernist can do this better than the Conservative, I want to be a Modernist. My leanings are toward the Conservative interpretation of the Bible and the Constructive believers in the Savior. If we live with more faith and preach with more power... everybody who is seeking the best faith will want ours. The test of divinity is in the saving power of our gospel, not Apostolic succession but Apostolic success. (7)

A Call to the Colors was another tract written by Dr. Wilson in 1933 on the critical need for a revival of genuine religion. He began with a quote from The Nation magazine: "We are now living in a bankrupt world," and a quote from Collier's with a "call for the church to get back to God." "Shall the underworld have the upper hand?" asked Dr. Wilson. It was his view that the legalizing of liquor was a movement to put money ahead of men. He saw in the ending of Prohibition a whole Congress swept away by love for money.

Hope was to be found in God and religion. Yet the church was lacking in the intense Christian life. There was little vital preaching to be found. It was a period of "highbrow" objection to emotion in religion. Only religion was to be circumspect and lifeless. "In sports we call emotional persons fans. In religion we call them fanatics." Dr. Wilson went on to attack fads of the day. First was the fad of the rural church. Most of the rural church advocates had not been near a rural church, believed Dr. Wilson. A second fad was to educate persons into the church in place of converting degenerate souls.

> The process of changing from sin to sainthood is from above. You cannot create a metaphysical entity by moral processes or educate a bad man into a good one by human means, that transformation is the work of God. (8)

And so Dr. Wilson held firm to the orthodox views he had been taught from childhood and attempted as best he could to withstand the rising tide of modernism within the church he loved so dearly.

The Case for Prohibition was a book written by Dr. Wilson and Deets Pickett in 1929. This book contained an informative history of the Prohibition movement, a statement of its accomplishments, a study of its effects on American prosperity, a series of outstanding opinions on its benefits, and a prophecy of its future. The whole case for Prohibition was stated conclusively by two men who had become its leading advocates.

In the waning years of national Prohibition, the book was intended to convince right-thinking and fair-minded people that Prohibition was a policy of value to the country as a whole; that it has contributed largely to the raising of the standard of living and the happiness of the masses; that it is essential to the best interest of legitimate trade; that only greed and selfishness or a total lack of comprehension of the facts led anyone to desire its destruction.

It was the author's view that Prohibition stood shoulder to shoulder with peace as the twin giants who could solve the world's problems. The one obstacle to worldwide prohibition was the failure of the people to realize the enormity of the drink waste. (9) "Prohibition cannot stop because it has conscience behind it. It will encircle the globe and spread its mantle of prosperity and happiness over every land." (10) This was the visionary view held forth by the authors as they made their case for Prohibition.

Dr. Wilson had considerable interest in governmental affairs. His view that the Constitution of the United States was Biblically inspired was set forth in a book published in 1922, entitled *The Divine Right of Democracy*. The book was dedicated as follows: "To my wife, inspirer of my plans and companion of my toils, who has helped me to live what I herein teach—Democracy." (11)

Chapter One is devoted to the thesis that the Hebrew scriptures, the law of Moses, and the teachings of Christ were the forgotten sources of the United

States Constitution. The Bible was the one book known to the founding fathers of this country. Dr. Wilson pointed to Washington taking his oath of office with the Bible in his hand. Judges and executives all promised to enforce laws upon that Book. "The weekly observance of the Lord's Day, the celebration of all the days of Christ—as Easter and Christmas—the annual observance of Thanksgiving and prayer in times of national distress, the sentiment on every dollar with which we pay our debts, 'In God We Trust,' proclaims with the Supreme Court of the land that 'this is a Christian nation.' (12)

"But above these when our fathers met to form a new government they copied every principle and modeled every plan from that ancient government, when God alone was King . . . While monarchy was supreme in all other governments for 470 years Israel had no king. The rule of kings is the rule of ruin. God made man for self-government."

Dr. Wilson points to the two most colossal blunders of government. The first heresy is that a royal family or a fictitious line of demarcation be established between ruler and his people. The second heresy is the law of primogeniture, which implies that the eldest son of the royal family is born with the ruler's prerogative. In Dr. Wilson's view, the American idea of selecting rulers by merit and not by birthright is from Scripture. "The Hebrew Bible ignores the universal custom and blazes a trail of independence." (13)

Chapter Two deals with the building of American democracy into government. It is a fictitious view that "the king's mind is the only law. But our fathers, studying their Bibles and feeling the common instincts of human nature, turned away from all this subterfuge and determined to found a nation on the fitness of mankind for self-government." (14) Dr. Wilson saw the laws of God as the foundation of our common law. He found a remarkable parallel between the divinely given Ten Commandments and the laws of the modern democracies. Gideon declined the offer to be king; likewise, George Washington refused to be called king.

Chapter Three is devoted to Jesus Christ as the embodiment of democratic ideas. "Jesus could not preach the doctrine of God's Fatherhood without reverting to human brotherhood... Jesus built Christianity on the doctrines of race, quality, and human brotherhood. When Jesus came to deal with the people his favorite term for himself was "The Son of man,"... Not "The Son of a king." (15) "Jesus was 'the sower who went forth to sow.' He planted the seed of democracy from which sprang the great tree of human liberty ... How? By giving man a new sense of the capacities, the relations, the duties, and the destiny of man ... and Jesus by the very act of selecting twelve apostles declared that the humblest person was equal to the highest things. (16) The chapter ends with a comparison of the lofty ideas of our Declaration of Independence to the fundamental doctrines of the New Testament.

Chapter Four poses the question, "Is Uncle Sam a Christian?" A review is made of the Christian conscience that formed this nation. Noah Webster is quoted: "The United States commenced their existence under circumstances wholly novel and unexampled in the history of nations. They commenced with civilization, with learning, with science, with art, with a constitution of government, and with the best gift of God to man, the Christian religion." (17) "Our nation is classed among the nations of the world as a Christian republic. It was settled by Christians who came to glorify God and extend the influence of the Christian religion." (18)

In the next chapter Dr. Wilson addresses the pagan inroads on American democracy. Some were calling Germany a pagan land at the time of the First World War. "Germany is not a pagan land; she is a Christian nation secularized, or, as the Methodists would say, "back-slidden." (19) A nation that had been the most Christian nation in Europe had been corrupted by the process called "higher criticism" to undermine the faith of the people and the integrity of the Bible. (20) "They banished the Bible from the public school systems, turned the Sabbath into a Continental Sunday of beer-drinking, gambling, and brutal pleasures ... and made beer the national beverage." (21)

"The civilized world... is trying to throw off the ideals of German rationalism... Why? Because the race stand appalled in the presence of the fruit that grew on that tree ... Their rationalized Christ is not our Savior. Their crazy-quilt Bible is not our Holy Scripture."

It was Dr. Wilson's desire that Uncle Sam face the stairway down which Germany ran to ruin and put his feet on every one of those steps —and walk over them in the opposite direction—upstairs. (22)

Dr. Wilson called for the strictest respect for and enforcement of law. An appeal was made for a total abstinence pledge-signing campaign. He called for an educational and moral persuasion campaign against the use of cigarettes. He called for the Bible, the whole Bible, to be taught once again in the public schools. He called for the observance of the American Sabbath as a day of rest and an opportunity for worship. He spoke up for the establishment of red-light abatement laws in every city and state, the teaching of old-fashioned American morality as standard for both men and women, and a pure American home life.

Dr. Wilson continued his list of upward steps by calling for "a strong push on the wheels of the anti-prizefighting movement." He said it was time to clean up the moving picture industry. "We must be involved in a great anti-gambling crusade." He called for withdrawing the protection of the American flag from citizens who go to any foreign country to engage in a traffic, or to set up an institution which has been outlawed by the Constitution and statutes of the United States. The chapter ends by stating, "This is a Christian nation. In this nation the Church of Christ has a supreme task. She should stand with any who faithfully execute our laws, fight for him as long as he keeps these standards, and turn against him and his party if they abandon the right and fail to serve the people and their government." (23)

Chapter Six is devoted to the function of law in civil government. British jurist William Blackstone is quoted as saying, "A law that contravenes the law of God or a law of nature is no law at all." In Dr. Wilson's view the object of human law was to enforce the laws of nature. The source of all progress is found in law and its penalty, believed Dr. Wilson. "Law to the obedient means protection. Penalty to the disobedient begets fear."

"Law is a rule of action," says Blackstone.

'The law of the Lord is perfect," says the psalmist.

'The law is a tutor to bring us unto Christ," says Paul. (24)

> Laws in all human governments are designed for protection and education, and they accomplish their purposes only as they are obeyed or enforced. When no law is made no penalty can exist, and where there is no penalty there is no fear, and when there is no fear education has failed of results. (25)

Dr. Wilson was a strong advocate for capital punishment. "One of the most notorious defects in our civilization is the utter inadequacy of our criminal law and its administration to prevent murder." (26) "We think a careful investigation will show that wherever the death penalty for murder is relaxed murders will multiply." (27)

Dr. Wilson had a great love for Oregon, his adopted home state. The final chapter of *The Divine Right of Democracy*, titled 'The Latest Evolution of American Democracy," is a tribute to the constitutional government of the State of Oregon. "The State of Oregon was founded by missionaries. It was built on the foundation of the Bible and church, schools, and homes." (28) Dr. Wilson viewed the modern system of government as the purest of civilizations with the highest moral standards and the freest popular government of any state in the union or country of the world. (29) "The Australian ballot system was tried out there and passed on to the other States. The direct primary nominations were inaugurated in Oregon and have since been adopted elsewhere. The anomaly of allowing United States senators to be elected for the people by proxy was wiped off the map in Oregon, and a direct method of permitting the people to select their own senators was tried on, made good, and finally was embodied in the Federal Constitution, so that every State in the union could follow Oregon's lead. (30)

"In Oregon the people secured the direct primary and adopted the initiative, referendum, and the recall, so that they could select their own leaders, write their own laws, repeal those that ought to be changed, and call back from office those whom they had trusted and who had proved unworthy." (31) Dr. Wilson simply could not boast enough about Oregon. "We have the best State government and the best governed cities, with the freest expression of the popular will and the highest type of Christian civilization to be found under our flag." (32) "In all this modern movement to put the power of government back in the hands of the people, Oregon has been a leader. Her initiative and referendum became the keystone of the arch of popular government." (33) Dr. Wilson concludes his book by writing:

> Let us not stay or hinder popular government on its road to the throne of power, but

> aid to our utmost that evolution in our system which links every department, legislative, judicial, and executive indissolubly with the power that is responsible for it, the people themselves. In the complicated needs and perplexities of our time every State in our Union ought to have the whole Oregon system of reforms, "that government of the people, by the people, and for the people, shall not perish from the earth." (34)

Perhaps as clear a picture as any of the world as Dr. Wilson saw it was his article for *The Forum* magazine in June 1935. It seems a fitting conclusion to this chapter.

THE WORLD AS I WANT IT
By Clarence True Wilson

> *This is the best world I have ever been in, yet! I like its health, its scenery, its opportunities, and its people. When they go right I admire them and when they go wrong I feel quite at home with them.*
>
> *I'd like to see depressions ended, wars stopped, race hatreds eliminated, and the liquor traffic, which now seeks to engulf us, forever annihilated. Some people changed their minds about that matter. Mine has been confirmed by the promises broken, by the same old deeds of iniquity perpetrated by the same unprincipled gang. They are selling poison to men, women, and children now and to little*

tots they are peddling candy that contains a quarter of a teaspoonful of strong liquor in every chocolate drop. They are running for a fall.

I believe in governments. Any government is better than none. But I would cut the price of government to one third of what it now is and then reduce it a little annually. We are headed wrong when we are making a paternity to take care of all who are willing to be carried and nursed. Excessive taxes break down respect for government and bring on hatred of it. We are heading that way now.

I would like to live in a world where men are religious and intense believers but believe as intensely in the other man's right to his own religion.

I'd like to see primary education universal; but I think purposeless college education useless. We have made a fad of educating people who neither need it nor can carry it.

Give us a world where men believe in God and live, therefore, as brothers; where nations settle their disputes as decent individuals do—by reason or arbitration; where men recognize human liberty as essential but will not tolerate big fortunes made by robbery or vice or by poisoning their fellow men—a world of leadership where they do not follow a multitude to do evil...

I am a great believer in the joys of country life as expounded and elaborated upon by Cicero in his De Senectute. I'd like to live out of doors, where I could enjoy flowers and fields and cattle, sheep and goats, horses and ponies. I'd rather associate with thorough-bred horses than with scrub people. What takes the joy out of life is the clock-like schedule for work and the abnormal hours for fun that have grown up with our city dwellers. This rush is carried over into leisure and has stepped up its tempo to such a pace that it is no longer leisure; it becomes strenuous and it leads to all sorts of abnormalities in social life.

The world I would like to live in would always have a majority of the people living on the soil instead of on cobblestones; they would be living in their own houses (It is hard to make a home out of a flat)—a world of homes with just enough government to prevent evildoers from robbing or molesting the law-abiding and the true. A world of love and friendship and tolerance, instead of bigotry and narrowness, would be worth living in. I'd like to try it for a thousand years.(35)

The angel who makes record of the annals of the temperance reform will be compelled to write in large and shinning letters the name of Clarence True Wilson.

— 12 —

Back in Oregon: The Restful Years (1936-1939)

The 1936 Methodist General Conference marked the end of Dr. Wilson's tenure as General Secretary of the Board of Temperance, Prohibition, and Public Morals, as' well as a turn in direction for the denomination. It was recommended that a new Secretary of the Board be appointed by the General Conference and not by the Board of Temperance. Dr. Wilson requested retirement and helped with the plan for restructuring. On May 13,1936, at age 64, Dr. Wilson requested the General Conference to grant him and Mrs. Wilson "a more restful life" in retirement.

Bishop Edwin Holt Hughes praised Dr. Wilson's work and requested that Dr. Clarence True Wilson be elevated to position of "Secretary Emeritus" by action of the General Conference. This action was passed and Dr. Ernest H. Cherrington was elected Executive Secretary of the Board of Temperance.

Bishop Hughes ended his remarks by saying:

> *"Few men have built such a monument as Dr. Wilson's work now bequeaths to us in the capital of our nation. He was as intrepid in his*

efforts to secure our magnificent property as he was in his public presentations of our cause. We would multiply gracious and true words concerning a work that began without a typewriter or a dollar for salary, until it comes to this hour with an equity that represents over and far more than one million dollars.

"I end this statement with an expression of the conviction common to us all, namely, that the angel who makes record of the annals of the temperance reform will be compelled to write in large and shining letters the name of Clarence True Wilson."

The audience arose and applauded.

Harold Paul Sloan made the motion that Dr. Wilson be elected to the position of Secretary Emeritus: "In view of Dr. Wilson's action asking for release from his very heavy labors, I would like to make the motion that he be accorded the position of Secretary Emeritus in the Board of Temperance. I feel that everyone in this General Conference, especially after the response you made both to Dr. Wilson's and Bishop Hughes' eloquent remarks, recognizes the creative service ren-dered by this great knight of a great reform.

"It will interest you to know that in the past few months he had brought to pass the coming into possession of the Board of more than $100,000—the money is not yet in; I mean the prospect of it—toward the reduction of the debt on that great building of ours facing the Capitol in Washington. So I would like to move, as

a recognition to him, that we create him Secretary Emeritus."

Roy L. Smith continued the praise of Dr. Wilson: "I would like to have the honor of seconding that motion, and making this very brief comment.

"Some years ago it was my privilege to be in attendance at the Conference of the Irish Church meeting that time in Cork, and an old man in the midst of the testimony service arose and said, years ago when I was a young man entering the ministry I promised the good Lord that every time I left my house I would make the devil sorry before I go back.' There is no man in the Methodist Church who has thrown more terror into the ranks of the traffickers in alcohol in the last twenty-five years than Clarence True Wilson. We pay him this tribute."

Bishop Blake, who was presiding, then said to the Conference: "If you will adopt the motion offered by Dr. Sloan and seconded by Dr. Smith, and elect Dr. Clarence True Wilson Secretary Emeritus of your Board of Temperance, Prohibition, and Public Morals, you will lift the hand; opposed, if any. The motion is adopted." (1)

The 1936 Conference marked the beginnings of a new direction regarding social concerns for the denomination. The delegates voted a moderate policy of social action. It was "a middle-of-the-road stand on social and economic questions." A declaration was read by Bishop-elect G. Bromley Oxnam of Depauw University. "The declaration upheld the right of the Church to be heard on social and economic questions, but repulsed any attempt to encourage Communism or Fascism. In the presence of hunger, injustice, and exploitation we insist it is not only the right of the Church to speak, but its bounden duty." The Methodist Federation for Social Service had asked the church to recommend "substitution of a planned social economy for the profit-seeking system." (2)

While the Methodist Episcopal Church was moving in new directions, the Wilsons were returning home to Oregon to retire at their farm near Gresham. The board provided their expenses for a steamship trip through the Panama Canal on this final trip from Washington, D.C., to Oregon. Dr. Wilson enjoyed visits on the ship with a variety of interesting persons. One visit was with a Jewish woman. He never failed to get acquainted with a wide range of individuals. Among his friends, due to his interest in livestock, was J. C. Penney, who also raised livestock.

The following winter on February 27,1937, Dr. Wilson was stricken by a cerebral hemorrhage. His condition was listed as "very serious." However Dr. Wilson managed a remarkable recovery from that illness.

Dr. Wilson, along with Wayne Wheeler, had been considered "the unofficial power of the Prohibition era." "The events of Dr. Wilson's career marked him as one of the most prominent and militant Methodist preachers in the United States. There perhaps is not a state in the Union in which he has not agitated and fought for Prohibition." Dr. Wilson had lost five months of work over the fours years prior to retirement due to poor health. He said, "I will continue to help but not to lead."

In retirement Dr. Wilson devoted time to his support of the Anglo-Saxon Federation. He wished for better health so he could give greater support for the work of the group. The Federation was an organization of persons interested in the study and promotion of the doctrine that the ten lost tribes of Israel are found in the Anglo-Saxon race. (3)

Following the repeal of Prohibition and Dr. Wilson's retirement, he and other Prohibition leaders were quickly forgotten. A reader wrote one of the newspapers in the mid-1930s asking, "What has become of Bishop Cannon and Clarence True Wilson?" The answer was as follows:

> *In 1934 the Methodist Episcopal Church South's General Board of Temperance and Social Welfare, headed by Bishop Cannon, was merged with the M. E. Church to become the Methodist Church by the General Conference of the Church. Bishop Cannon still maintains a business address at 131 B Street, S.E., Washington, D.C., and a legal residence in Blackstone, Virginia.*
>
> *Rev. Clarence True Wilson, from 1910 until 1936 head of the Board of Temperance, Prohibition, and Public Morals of the Methodist Episcopal Church, suffered a heart attack and general breakdown in 1934. He resigned his position in May, 1936, and retired to his farm*

at Gresham, near Portland, Oregon, where he devotes his time to his hobbies—the simplification of spelling, cattle breeding, and the propagation of the theory that John Wilkes Booth, Lincoln's assassin, es-caped the soldiers sent to kill him and died an old man under an assumed name." (4)

The people of the little town of Gresham were fascinated that such a famous person had retired there. From time to time the *Gresham Outlook*, as well as Portland papers, carried articles about Dr. Wilson. One such article from the Outlook is reprinted here:

Living quietly on a hillside several miles southwest of Gresham on Heiney Road is Gresham's most distinguished citizen, Dr. Clarence True Wilson, who for 26 years served as executive secretary of the Board of Temperance, Prohibition, and Public Morals of the Methodist Episcopal Church, with headquarters in Washington, D.C. Dr. Wilson retired a year ago to his farm home, from which is visible a gorgeous panorama taking in the valley between Gresham and Portland, the fringe of mountains bordering the Columbia River on the north and on a clear day, Mt. St. Helens, Mt. Adams, and Mt. Rainier in the distance. Surrounded by a wealth of natural beauty, Dr. Wilson reminisces over a life which represents a tremendous outpouring of energy.

It is no idle guess to say that this militant temperance worker has in his life delivered more speeches than any living man. In all parts of the United States he has lectured before audiences of all kinds, ranging in size from a few dozen to ten or twelve thousand.

Comparing notes with William Jennings Bryan, Dr. Wilson found that he had given two or three speeches to every one given by "the great commander." For a period of ten years he spoke an average of 1000 times a year.

Dr. Wilson varied his lectures by arranging debates with men of public affairs who held views on opposite sides of controversial issues. He has participated in such public forums with 30 different men during his life, many of them nationally prominent. For a period of five years he traveled and debated with Clarence Darrow, noted criminal lawyer, on the Prohi-bition question.

It is a remarkable thing that Dr. Wilson afterward became the personal friend of every man against whom he debated. Just a few days before this interview he had received a letter from Darrow, now living in Chicago, one of seven from his former platform opponent since his recent illness.

Mention of Darrow brought a reference to the famous Scopes trial in Tennessee some years back when the clever attorney humiliated William Jennings Bryan, already a broken man. Bryan was attempting to enjoin Scopes from the teaching of evolution in high school, making the point that so long as religion was no longer taught, anti-religion ought not be taught either. Although Bryan was awarded the case he suffered tremendously at the hands of the cynical Darrow and the effects of the trial hurried his death, Dr. Wilson believes. Darrow is regarded by Dr. Wilson as one of the most interesting and versatile men in America.

Not the least of Dr. Wilson's achievements was the raising of funds for construction of the Methodist building in Washington, D.C., a $2,000,000 structure located across from the capitol. In it are housed apartments, some of them occupied by congressmen and supreme court justices, a beautiful restaurant and lobby, the headquarters of the Methodist bishop, district superintendent, and members of the board of which Dr. Wilson is now secretary emeritus. The huge structure is mostly paid for and yields an annual income used for work of the board.

Asked whether he thought a Prohibition law would come back, Dr. Wilson replied that conditions now were so insufferably bad that the decent people of the country would eventually wake up and bring it back to stay. Conditions now, in some respects, are worse than they were before Prohibition, he said.

Dr. Wilson would like to get back into the fight for reform, but he is warned by his physicians that it would be fatal. Last February he suffered a stroke which paralyzed one whole side and rendered him speechless. His rapid recovery he regards as no less than miraculous. He attributes it to the skill of Gresham doctors and the prayers of his thousands of friends. He declares that he is now in better physical condition that he has been any time in the last five years.

Living in a spot as near heavenly as earth can provide Dr. Wilson is enjoying a well earned respite from a lifetime of earnest toil devoted to the cause of uplift. Although his active work is stopped, his influence lives in the minds and hearts of men and women all over the nation." (5)

In April 1937, Dr. Wilson received word that his dear friend and colleague in temperance reform work, Bishop William Fraser McDowell, had died, Tuesday, April 27, at the age of 79. Bishop McDowell had served as resident bishop in Chicago from 1904 to 1916 and in Washington, from 1916 to 1932. He served for many years as president of the Methodist Board of Temperance. He was characterized by his associates as "the supreme Preacher of the Methodist denomination." "McDowell was progressive in religious thought. . . yet many of his most intimate friends were conservatives," said Dr. Wilson. (6)

A year later, March 13, 1938, Dr. Wilson's close friend, Clarence Darrow, died at age 80. "I've fought all my life for the underdog," said Darrow. He outlined his philosophy of life by saying, "My greatest satisfaction has been my efforts in behalf of the unfortunates." And his greatest task had been "trying my hardest to help overcome the cruelties of the world." From the year 1925 to 1935 Dr. Wilson and Darrow had debated forty-six times. "I feel lonely to think he is gone," said Dr. Wilson. (7)

The May 16, 1938, issue of *Unity* magazine was devoted entirely to memorial tributes to Clarence Darrow. Among the tributes was one by Clarence True Wilson.

CLARENCE DARROW AS A FRIEND
Clarence True Wilson

On Sunday, March 13, 1938, there passed off the stage of action one of the most brilliant, witty, sincere, and true men, the greatest criminal lawyer of our age, and the most colorful personality we have had since Theodore Roosevelt and William Jennings Bryan passed on. My close association for the last ten years has taught me to respect him, admire his personality, and enjoy his companionship. The world seems lonesome without him. I had forty-six joint debates on the Prohibition question in as many cities and in thirty states. I have had three or four religious debates and one on capital punishment. Collier's sent us as opponents, together to Canada, to write up from our different viewpoints impressions of the liquor situation there. While I differed from him on many points, I came to admire him and to love him.

It was not always so. If there was any man I reprobated in American life, it was Clarence Darrow. He had defended most of the men I "knew" ought to be executed. When the Ohio "drys" wired me to come and debate prohibi-

tion with Clarence Darrow, I eagerly accepted, glad to get at him. In a conversation, I learned that he was bitterly opposed to capital punishment, believed that the State had no more right to take a human life than he had. He therefore could consistently try to save the life of any man who asked him to defend him; so one prejudice was done.

His ideas of the government were less strict than mine; he therefore never prosecuted anyone in his life. Always defending, he was naturally against restrictive laws, and for liberty, bridled or unbridled. He was therefore against local option, Prohibition, and any restrictive measures on the liquor traffic. Not agreeing with him, I agreed that he was sincere. In five years of those joint debates, I learned that he was fair, on given point, he acknowledged it graciously.

I was invited out to dinner with him innumerable times. He never made his habits embarrass me in any way. When he drank wine, he preferred to do it privately, but he was abstemious both in eating and drinking. I constantly enjoyed his witticisms and his humorous conversation. When we were debating in Portland, my home city, my wife's family and mine came down to see us off. I thought I would like to introduce Mr. Darrow to them after the debate of that night. I presented the folks and their children. He looked up in a quizzical way and said, "I knew you packed the house for me tonight." When Mr. Darrow made the first address, he indulged in so much humor that he got the audience hilarious and then hysterical. At the close of his funny speech, making Prohibition the butt of ridicule—and the Prohibitionists also—I remarked: "We have a tacit agreement that Mr. Darrow will furnish all the fun and repartee, and get the laughter and applause, while he depends upon me to furnish all the facts and the arguments, and take the votes." After I had done my best to make good, Darrow responded, "The doctor has told you that I am to furnish the fun and he the facts and arguments; well, ladies and gentlemen, I have done my best to make good on that, why in thunder doesn't he do his part?" This was so much enjoyed by the audience that I put this in again and again so as to give him a chance to come back at me with this fine joke, too good to be missed. When we traveled across the continent and visited eleven cities, our wives accompanied us, so that the four of us traveled together. I do not think any four people ever enjoyed themselves more, or were more agreeable. Once we were sitting opposite in the pullman and Mrs. Darrow innocently remarked, "Dr. Wilson, you have blue eyes, haven't you? I never noticed it before until you were sitting in that light." I was slowly thinking of what to say (I had never had to account for my eyes before), when Darrow, quick-witted as usual, responded, "Mrs. Wilson, I have been traveling around with you and your husband for two weeks, and you have never said a word about my eyes yet."

I could fill chapters with these kinds of humorous remarks, that showed how he could oil the machinery of a court room, and of government as well. Many people think he did it by sledge-hammering, but they were mistaken. He did it by geniality, humor, and unanswerable arguments, so that the judge, the jury, the courtroom, and the witnesses fell in love with him, as I did debating with him. His creed and mine differed. He was an agnostic, while I was a believer, but I have never known any human being with whom I loved to discuss religion as I did with him. He was so frank, so open-minded, so eager to know the Christian viewpoint, and had so many Christian characteristics in his make-up that it did not matter so much about his creed.

Some years ago he was going to Europe to spend two or three months at one of the greatest resorts for health and pleasure on that continent. He confided to me that he was going to write a book on Christianity as he saw it. I said, "Well, Mr. Darrow, I think I know what you're going to do, and I'll say to you, make it strong. We deserve, we Christians, every word you'll give us of criticism. You'll not do justice to the job even at your best. I suppose we will be conscious of our shortcomings and pick up your book, and say we deserve every word of it, but when you have got your strongest chapter and reached your climax, don't stop there, but take Jesus of Nazareth, the Son of Man, and tell us the truth about him. That he wasn't a hypocrite, he wasn't selfish, he wasn't a coward, he was not two-faced, he was not inconsistent, he didn't profess one thing and miss the mark about every time. When you have given us Christians a good drubbing, give the Savior of the World His just dues as a compensation." "Well," he said, "I'll take your advice on that, and put my last chapter on Jesus." I did not see him for six months. I asked him how he got along with his book. He said, "D____ you, you spoiled my book. I have never written a word of it."

We visited in each other's homes. One time we were having a delightful feast at his table. Looking at my watch and seeing that 7:45 had arrived, I said in a startled way, "I have an engagement tonight to preach for the Holiness people down at the Chicago Evangelistic Training School, and I must go at once." He said," What do you mean by holiness?" I replied, "Well, the word holiness is a contraction of the word wholeness. These people believe that the great fault of us Chris-tians is not that we fail to hit the mark, but that we do not even put our standards high enough. They insist that we must love the Lord, our God, with all our heart, soul, mind, and strength, and our neighbors as ourselves; in other words, that we shall make a whole-hearted consecration of all we have and are to the service of Christ." "Well," said Mr. Darrow, "If I were a Christian at all, that is the kind of a Christian

I should want to be." Quite a tribute from one of the brainiest men in our country to the radical type of Christian leaders who go the whole limit of service and sacrifice, surrender, and devotion to their religious ideals.

He told me about seeing John Brown, having him place his hand on his head as a little boy and saying, "Clarence, always be good and kind to the colored person. He has so few friends that he can't afford to lose two, you and me," and he always was devoted to the colored man's struggle to get on in the world. When Dr. Sweet, in Detroit, killed a white man who was in the mob trying to smash up his home, Darrow volunteered his services and defended him against an avalanche of prejudice, and cleared him. Sometimes, when men do things for others, they are surprised by the world's ingratitude. It makes them almost regret their services, but it was no exception to this rule to watch the Negro porters, the Negro waiters, and any other Negroes, who saw Mr. Darrow. They reverenced him, and showed it by their eager faces, the greatest gratitude I have ever seen displayed toward a benefactor. If kindness, brotherly love, sympathy for the downtrodden, taking up for the underdog, bearing one another's burdens are Christian traits, Mr. Darrow had the Christian ethics without the Christian's creed. (8)

Dr. Clarence True Wilson himself became critically ill on January 28, 1939, and died February 16,

1939, a few weeks short of his 67th birthday. His name was linked with the rise and fall of Prohibition in America. He died believing that Prohibition would one day be restored. Dr. Wilson's career was one of color, activity, and motion. He inherited his evangelical fervor with which he crusaded against liquor from his father. In the minds of many, the temperance movement represents the high-water mark of Methodist influence in national affairs in the twentieth century. True or not, Dr. Wilson's significance in American Methodist history can hardly be overrated.

Social progress demands we seek with a questioning mind to learn lessons from history to reflect upon the mistakes and progress there made, and seek for new truths yet to be revealed.

Postscript

Mark Twain once said, "A temperance speaker is like a body at a wake. Everybody hopes neither one will say very much." Hopefully, I haven't said too much regarding the life and times of temperance crusader Clarence True Wilson. How necessary that the lives and times of past heroes not be forgotten. "Those who cannot remember the past are condemned to repeat it," said George Santayana.

Harry Emerson Fosdick in his autobiography, *The Living of These Days*, dismissed the whole temperance/Prohibition movement in a page and a half:

> The endeavor to deal with the liquor problem by a prohibitory amendment to the federal Constitution I watched with foreboding, as it rose to furious intensity during World War I and then, after a transient victory, petered out. I never believed in Prohibition ... I believed in local option but not in what the Prohibitionists were fighting for. In January, 1919, however, the Eighteenth Amendment was passed, and a year later it was put into active operation. Along with many others, I saw nothing to do except to back it up and try to make a success of it. I certainly tried hard, endeavoring to see all the good I could in it,

> pleading for the observance of the law, and wanting desperately to avoid the setback and disillusionment bound to follow the breakdown of so well-intentioned an effort to destroy the liquor traffic. In one sermon ... I stated my judgment that "such sumptuary legislation, written into the Constitution," was a "mistake in strategy," and I expressed regret that this "peremptory handling of the liquor question has undoubtedly landed us in an unsatisfactory position." What happened is notorious history now. There are some things that federal legislation cannot do. (1)

Over the next half century, Methodism was to move on to other pressing social issues, nearly forsaking the alcohol problem—leaving it for others to solve. When I entered Boston University School of Theology in the fall of 1958, Dr. Martin Luther King, Jr., had just completed his doctorate and was already at the helm of the civil rights movement. This and the anti-war movement were to take up the attention of the church and society of the fifties and the sixties. Later, in the seventies and eighties, women's issues and gay rights issues were to demand much of the attention of the social activists.

In 1972, I was appointed to the Sunnyside United Methodist Church in Portland, Oregon, just a few blocks from where Dr. Wilson had preached at the beginning of the century. During those years at Sunnyside, I became directly involved with the social movements that created tension within the church and the larger community. It was at that time I met the Rev. Mark Chamberlain, who had served for a number of years as executive secretary of the controversial Methodist Federation for Social Action. Mark kept the Federation alive during the years when Senator Joe McCarthy was leading the attack on all types of left-wing organizations. Mark's followers were mostly unchurched persons, some members of the Communist Party and other left-wing organizations. He had become a spiritual advisor to this little band of "political heretics." Someone once asked me if Mark was a Communist. I replied, "So far as his politics are concerned, I am not certain, but I do know he is as fine and dedicated a Christian as I have ever met."

I visited often with Mark and his wife, Dr. Corraine Chamberlain, at their country home less than a mile from the Wilson home place near Gresham. I had wondered if the Wilsons and the Chamberlains had known each other. This proved unlikely as the Chamberlains did not move to Oregon from Wisconsin until 1944. If Dr. Wilson had lived to the age of 90 or more, they would have known each other, and my guess is they would have been the best of friends. Dr. Wilson, the conservative Republican; Chamberlain, the left-wing advocate. Both coming to their politics out of a deep Biblical faith. Mark Chamberlain would have been in complete agreement with Dr. Wilson on temperance issues. Mark continued to see temperance reform as an essential part of the social gospel. He was troubled when alcohol was served at Federation gatherings. Likewise, he could not understand the Federation's stand in support of gay rights.

How I would have enjoyed sitting in on a conversation between Dr. Wilson and Chamberlain. This, however, was not to be, due to Dr. Wilson's premature death. However, through my position as executive director of Oregonians Concerned about Addiction Problems, I have become an affiliate member of the American Council on Alcohol Prob-lems. In that organization I find some who still have the spirit and enthusiasm of the old-time temperance reformers. I went reluctantly to join their ranks, thinking them to be simply relics of the past. I have come to admire their courage and commitment even today to the cause of temperance. What a contrast to the lukewarm Christianity so often practiced in the church. Through them I have gained a glimpse of the kind of men and women who crusaded for temperance reform and Prohibition. For we are indeed "surrounded by so great a cloud of witnesses." (2)

Social progress demands we seek with a questioning mind to learn lessons from history, to reflect upon the mistakes and progress there made, and seek for new truths yet to be revealed. It is well to celebrate the life and times of Clarence True Wilson. With great energy and devotion he lived a life of prayer, study, speaking, and writing because he had compassion for those harmed by alcohol. He believed this terrible trouble could be solved through education and law enforcement. Valiant for the truth, he gave all that he had for what he believed to be true. Now we honor him, grieve the passing of that time in history, and seek, as he predicted we would, new answers to the alcohol and drug problems of our day.

Endnotes

Chapter 1: Ancestry and Youth (1872-1895)

1. Cyclopedia of Temperance.
2. Minutes, Wilmington Annual Conference, 1871.
3. From "The Fighter of Fairmount" by Clarence True Wilson.
4. Oregon Daily Journal, September 21, 1907.
5. Prohibition Leaders in America, 1895.
6. From unpublished Wilson papers.
7. The National Cyclopedia of American Biography, p. 136.
8. Prohibition Leaders in America, 1895.
9. From 1907 Promotional Brochure.
10. Ibid.
11. Oregon Daily Journal, September 21, 1907.

Chapter 2: From Delaware to California (1895-1904)

1. From History of School of Theology at Claremont.
2. Oregon Daily Journal, September 21, 1907.
3. From Wilson papers.

Chapter 3: Oregon Years (1905-1910)

1. Oregon Daily Journal, September 21, 1907.

2. Ibid.
3. Rev. Dr. Asa Sleeth in 1907 Promotional Brochure.
4. From Wilson papers.
5. Clark, Norman H., The Dry Years, Prohibition and Social Change in Washington State, p. 10.
6. Ibid. p. 29.
7. From Wilson papers.
8. Ibid.
9. Ibid.
10. Ibid.
11. Ibid.

Chapter 4: Chicago and Topeka Years (1910-1916)

1. Pickett, Deets, "Board of Temperance Report," General Conference Minutes, 1928.
2. Ibid.
3. From Wilson papers.
4. Report of the Flying Squadron.
5. Ibid.
6. Ibid.
7. Ibid.
8. Ibid.

Chapter 5: Move to Washington and Prohibition Victory (1916-1920)

1. Letter from Governor Arthur Capper, June 5, 1916.
2. The Voice, October 1916.
3. The Voice, July 1916.
4. Ibid.

5. From Wilson papers.
6. Ibid.
7. Ibid.
8. Yearbook of Churches and Agencies, 1917.
9. From Wilson papers.
10. Ribuff, Leo P., "Social Reform to the Great Depression," The History of American Methodism, Volume III, 1964, p. 1539.
11. From Wilson papers.
12. From Wilson papers.
13 The Advocate Journal, January 29, 1920.

Chapter 6: The Story of the Methodist Building

1. From Promotional Brochure.
2. From Report to Board by Mrs. Wilson.
3. Ibid
4. Ibid
5. Ibid
6. Ibid
7. Ibid

Chapter 7: Prohibition Years (1920-1933) From Triumph to Demise

1. Ribuff, op. cit, p. 1540.
2. From address by Clarence True Wilson, London, England, Septem-ber 15, 1921.
3. Pacific Christian Advocate, March 21, 1923.
4. From address by Clarence True Wilson, Santa Barbara, California, September 25, 1924.
5. Washington Star, December 6, 1924.
6. From Wilson papers.

7. The Adult Bible Class Monthly, August 1927.
8. From address by Clarence True Wilson, "What Has Prohibition Done?" December 6, 1927.
9. Plain Talk, March 1929.
10. Henning, Arthur Sears, "The Lobby," Liberty, April 6, 1929.
11. Ibid.
12. Editorial, New York Daily News, May 2, 1929.
13. Chicago Tribune, July 19, 1929.
14. Chicago Tribune, July 11, 1929.
15. Time, July 1, 1929.
16. New York Daily News, May 7, 1929.
17. World Service News, February 1930.
18. Ibid.
19. Tucker, Ray T. The North American Review, August 1930.
20. The Christian Century, December 1930, March 1931.
21. Dabney, Virginia, Dry Messiah, 1949, pp. 213-215,229.

Chapter 8: Darrow and Wilson: Best Friends

1. The Christian Advocate, March 27, 1930.
2. Baltimore Post, May 13, 1930.
3. From Wilson papers.
4. Universal Service, Baltimore, Maryland, May 14, 1930.
5. Detroit Evening Times, Detroit, Michigan, May 28, 1930.
6. Tribune, Great Falls, Montana, October 12, 1930.
7. Ibid.
8. From Wilson papers.

9. The Times, Seattle, Washington, October 15, 1930.
10. The Seattle Star, Settle, Washington, October 15, 1930.
11. Idaho Daily Statesman, Boise, Idaho, October 18, 1930.
12. Salt Lake Tribune, Salt Lake City, Utah, October 19, 1930.
13. Omaha Bee News, Omaha, Nebraska, October 22, 1930.
14. The Times, Kansas City, Missouri, October 24, 1930.
15. Milwaukee Sentinel, October 25, 1930.
16. Galveston Tribune, Galveston, Texas, November 5, 1930.
17. Galveston Daily, Galveston, Texas, November 6, 1930.
18. Houston Chronicle, Houston, Texas, November 7, 1930.
19. Houston Post-Dispatch, Houston, Texas, November 7, 1930.
20. Daily News, Washington, D.C., November 19, 1930.
21. A Birmingham, Alabama, newspaper, November 21, 1930.
22. Capital News, Boise, Idaho, October 10, 1930.
23. Ibid.
24. Ibid.
25. News Leader, Richmond, Virginia, December 7, 1932.

Chapter 9: Study of Ontario Liquor System

1. Wilson, Clarence True and Darrow, Clarence, "Clarence True Wil-son and Clarence Darrow Look at the Ontario Liquor System," Collier's, September 27, 1930.
2. Ibid.
3. Wilson, Clarence True, "And the Drinking Was According to t h e Law," Collier's, October 4, 1930.
4. Wilson, Clarence True, Twentieth Century Progress, November 1930.
5. Ibid.
6. Darrow, Clarence, "Let No Man Therefore Judge You in Meat or in Drink," Collier's, October 11, 1930.
7. Ibid.
8. Wilson, Clarence True, "Clarence Darrow as a Friend," Unity, May 16, 1938.

Chapter 10: Repeal: Bitter Aftertaste (1933-1936)

1. From Wilson papers.
2. Washington Post, Washington, D.C., December 5, 1933.
3. Letter from Clarence Darrow, March 23, 1933.
4. The National Voice, Los Angeles, California, January 4, 1934.
5. A Camden, New Jersey, newspaper, December 9, 1934.
6. The Lima News, Lima, Ohio, March 19, 1935.
7. The Seaford News, Seaford, Delaware, November 17, 1933.
8. The Star, Washington, D.C., December 26, 1933.

9. The Telegram, Youngstown, Ohio, March 4, 1935.
10. Ibid.
11. The Depository, Canton, Ohio, March 7, 1935.
12. The Daily News, Dayton, Ohio, April 3, 1935.
13. The Journal, Dayton, Ohio, April 3, 1935.
14. The Journal, Portland, Oregon, May 24, 1935.
15. The Union-Gazette, Newark, New Jersey, May 7, 1935.
16. The Gazette, Billings, Montana, June 17, 1935.
17. A Butte, Montana, newspaper, June 19, 1935.
18. Daily Independent, Helena, Montana, June 21, 1935.
19. Citizen, Columbus, Ohio, May, 1936.
20. The Washington Times, Washington, D.C., October 16, 1935.
21. Tribune-Gazette, New Hampton, Iowa, February 1, 1934.
22. Tribune, Blackwell, Oklahoma, October 18, 1934.
23. Town & Country Review, London, England, October 2, 1933.
24. From article on Wilson in Social Activists Series.

Chapter 11: Wilson the Writer

1. Wilson, Clarence True, Matthew Simpson: Patriot, Preacher, Prophet, 1929, p. 16.
2. Ibid. p. 24.
3. Ibid. p. 37.
4. Ibid. p. 40.
5. Ibid. p. 43.

6. Ibid. p. 44.

7. Wilson, Clarence True, What Ought the Consevative Do? 1931.
8. Wilson, Clarence True, A Call to the Colors, 1933.
9. Wilson, Clarence True and Pickett, Deets, The Case for Prohibition, 1929, p. 266.
10. Ibid. p. 273.
11. Wilson, Clarence True, The Divine Right of Democracy, 1922, Introduc-tion.
12. Ibid. pp. 15-16.
13. Ibid. pp. 16-23.
14. Ibid. p. 32.
15. Ibid. p. 49.
16. Ibid. p. 54.
17. Ibid. pp. 70-71.
18. Ibid. p. 71.
19. Ibid. p. 82.
20. Ibid. p. 83.
21. Ibid. p. 84.
22. Ibid. pp. 85-86.
23. Ibid. pp. 86-98.
24. Ibid. p. 103.
25. Ibid. p. 107.
26. Ibid. p. 113.
27. Ibid. p. 116.
28. Ibid. p. 118.
29. Ibid. p. 118.
30. Ibid. pp. 118-119.
31. Ibid. p. 119.
32. Ibid. p. 120.
33. Ibid. p. 128.

34. Ibid. pp. 139-140.
35. Wilson, Clarence True, "The World as I Want It," The Forum, New York, New York, June 1935, p. 375.

Chapter 12: Back in Oregon: The Restful Years (1936-1939)

1. General Conference Journal, 1936.
2. Ibid.
3. Gresham Outlook, Gresham, Oregon, June 26, 1936.
4. From Wilson papers.
5. Gresham Outlook, Gresham, Oregon, June 4, 1937.
6. Ibid.
7. Ibid.
8. Wilson, Clarence True, "Clarence Darrow as A Friend," Unity, May 16, 1938.

Postscript

1. Fosdick, Harry Emerson, The Living of These Days, pp. 288-289.
2. Hebrews 12:1 Revised Standard Version.

Notes

Notes

Notes

Notes

Notes